THE RIBBLE WAY

The Way crosses Thorns Gill, a pretty little limestone ravine, near Gearstones. (Section 8)

THE RIBBLE WAY

A 70 mile recreational footpath close to the
banks of the river from sea to source.

GLADYS SELLERS

ROUTE MAPS DRAWN BY JOHN WILSON PARKER
ILLUSTRATIONS BY R.BRIAN EVANS

Front Cover: The Ribble valley from the Way above Hothersall Hall.
Photo: Aileen Evans.
Back Cover: Dinckley Footbridge.

CICERONE PRESS
HARMONY HALL, MILNTHORPE, CUMBRIA

© Gladys Sellers 1985
ISBN 0902 363 697
First published 1985
Reprinted 1986

Contents

The Way in Detail:

ACKNOWLEDGEMENTS

I should like to express my sincere thanks to the following people: Mr. D.Sutherland and Mrs Alison Heine of the Lancashire County Council for many helpful conversations on progress and for providing me with detailed maps of the route in Lancashire; Mr. A.Neasham of the North Yorkshire County Council for his speedy assurances of action in that area and the provision of large scale maps of the right-of-way footpath diversions; Mr. R.Lonsdale of the Yorkshire Dales National Park for much useful information about path diversion orders and facilities within the Park; Mr.T.Clarkson and Mr. A.Howard of the Preston and Fylde Group of the Ramblers' Association for the history of the Ribble Way; Mr. N.Turner, Curator of the Castle Museum, Clitheroe, for a private tour of that Museum and for clarifying the geology of the Ribble Valley for me; and last but not least, Mrs Elsie Baines of Walton-le-dale for allowing me access to her extensive notes about Ribblesdale.

Gladys Sellers

*   *   *

Ribble Way

SECTIONS
shewn thus

Morecambe Bay

o Hawes

⌒ Dodd Fell

☐ SOURCE

Three Peaks

8

HORTON-IN-
RIBBLESDALE

o Stainforth

7

SETTLE

NORTH
YORKS.

Ingleton

o Lancaster

Forest
of
Bowland

6

Skipton

LANGS.

Hodder

5

GISBURN

o Sawley

BRUNGERLEY BR.

Wyre

Pendle

RIBCHESTER

Clitheroe

Calder

Burnley

Preston

3

4

PENWORTHAM
BR.

BROCKHOLES BR.

Lytham

1

2

Blackburn

Miles

Douglas

LONGTON

0   5   10

0   10   20

o Southport

⊙ Chorley

Kilometres

IRISH SEA

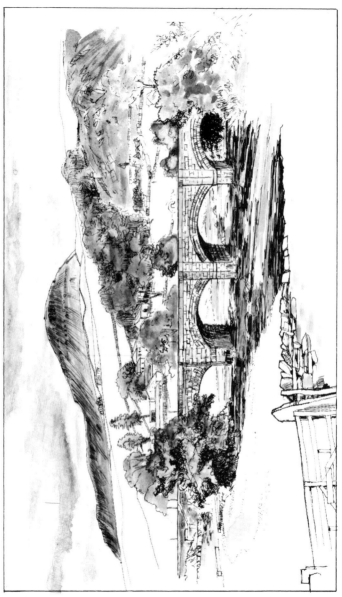

Pen-y-Ghent from the Way at Helwith Bridge. Here the Settle-Carlisle railway crosses the river.

THE WAY IN BRIEF

The Way starts at Longton, close to the river's mouth, and having joined the marsh banks, follows them and then the river embankment to Penwortham Bridge. It skirts the town of Preston through Broadgate, Miller and Avenham Parks, then follows the banks of the river to Brockholes Bridge. Here the Way leaves the river banks which it has followed to this point and cuts across country well above river level to the outskirts of Ribchester. From Ribchester the Way uses a circuitous field path to avoid a busy road and reaches the river bank again at the road bridge. It follows the river for about a mile and then climbs up to cut off a large bend and comes back to it at Dinckley Footbridge. Here the way crosses the bridge and continues well away from the river regaining it beyond Brockhole. After crossing the Calder by the new footbridge it reaches Great Mitton and continues, more or less on the river bank to Grindleton Bridge, Clitheroe. Soon after this bridge it leaves the river bank and does a short stretch on the road to regain the Ribble's bank just beyond Sawley, then follows the river through a superb wooded gorge almost to Gisburn. From the Bolton by Bowland road the Way goes cross country to Paythorne and Halton West, and does not regain the river bank, except briefly, until Settle. From Langcliffe the Way follows the bank except for one unfortunate stretch of road right to Horton in Ribblesdale. At Horton the route follows the pastures well above river level to Nether Lodge, then cuts direct over rough ground to Far Gearstones on the Ingleton-Hawes road. In order to avoid a busy road the Way now utilises the Dales Way as far as Newby Head, then follows Jam Sike to the source.

A return to Horton-in-Ribblesdale by the Pennine Way is suggested.

*   *   *

THE STORY OF THE RIBBLE WAY

The Ribble Way is without a doubt the brain child of the Preston and Fylde group of the Ramblers' Association, for at its inaugural meeting in 1967, the all important suggestion was made.

'We've got a Pennine Way,' they said, 'Why not work for a Ribble Way?' The idea was taken up with enthusiasm. There was no doubt that it was a worthwhile one because of the large numbers of people living close to the Ribble Valley.

The Valley was surveyed by members of the newly formed group in order to work out a route giving the best walking and, joined by members of the North East Lancashire Area of the Ramblers' Association in whose territory much of the route lay, they devised one that followed the banks of the Ribble from sea to Far Gearstones, a total of 64 miles. In many places right of way paths did not exist along the banks of the river so fishermen's paths were used, for they felt that to depart widely from the banks would lose the unique atmosphere of a riverside walk that was an essential part of the Ribble Way. The proposed route needed some 36 miles of new right of way paths. This early work took a great deal of time, and it was not until 1972 that the Ramblers were able to approach their national body with a proposal for the creation of a long distance footpath to be called The Ribble Way. The national body of the R.A. in turn approached the Countryside Commission and made a release to the Press. Not surprisingly the press release brought unfavourable comment and opposition from the Bowlands R.D.C. and from the National Farmers Union.

For several years very little happened until in 1980 the newly formed Mid Lancashire Area of the Ramblers' Association joined with the North East Lancashire Area to form a Ribble Way Committee. This committee set to work to devise a route which would be acceptable to the people who had objected so strongly to the original proposal. It was decided to shorten the route to end at Paythorne, close to the Lancashire County boundary. This meant that the whole of the route was now in Lancashire and in the territories of the two Ramblers' Association Areas concerned. This shortened route required only 19½ miles of new rights of way compared with the original proposal's 36. In March 1980 the Ribble Way Committee issued a proposal for The Ribble Way as a recreational footpath, describing the route in some detail, and in April 1980 the Countryside Commission convened a meeting to discuss their proposals. They invited the Lancashire branch of the N.F.U., the Country Landowners Association, Preston Borough

Council, South Ribble Borough Council, The Ribble Valley Borough Council, the Lancashire County Council, and obviously, the Mid Lancashire Area and North East Lancashire Area of the R.A. Again, there was considerable opposition by some of the bodies present though others were in favour, but it became clear that the establishment of the Ribble Way would depend on its using existing right of way paths almost entirely. For those who had worked so hard to open up the many fishermen's paths that gave such high quality walking this spelt defeat. More surveys were done and a composite route designed and called 'The Interim Ribble Way' signifying that all hope had not been abandoned even at this stage. The new route certainly offered compensations: there were excellent views up the valley that the riverside paths lacked.

In July 1982, as part of a nationwide campaign called 'Discover your local footpaths' organised by the national body of the R.A., the Interim Ribble Way was launched. R.A. members led a series of guided walks during the weekend of July 31st/August 1st to gain publicity for the scheme and sent letters to the Countryside Commission and the Lancashire County Council. Now the wheel of fortune changed: Officialdom expressed interest and eventually the Countryside Commission agreed to provide financial help while the Lancashire County Council undertook to carry out the work to improve stiles and footbridges where needed and to mark the route with the logo designed by a member of the Ribble Way Committee and displayed on the title page of this book. Before work started the Lancashire County Council held discussions with the Rambler's Association to make some minor modifications to the route. It was agreed that it should end at Gisburn, much better placed for public services than Paythorne, and to start at Longton to avoid expensive bridge works on the marsh banks required by the Much Hoole starting point. The original route walked the north bank of the Ribble between Ribchester and Great Mitton and required a new bridge over the Hodder at its junction with the Ribble and a subsequent mile or more of new right of way path. The alternatives were for people to walk the road, busy and dangerous, or to transfer the route to the south bank at Dinckley footbridge. This route required a bridge over the Calder but as it would be a less expensive structure than the proposed Hodder Bridge and as no new right of way paths were needed, this route was chosen. An opening ceremony by Mike Harding, President of Ramblers' Association and Sir Derek Barber, Chairman of the Countryside Commission took place on June 1st 1985 at Edisford Bridge, Clitheroe.

The Mid and North East Lancashire Areas of the Ramblers'

11

Association obviously hoped that this truncated Ribble Way would one day be extended to the original finishing point, but they accepted that this work would have to be undertaken by people living closer to the scene than their members.

In fact this extension was achieved much more speedily than expected. Cicerone Press gave the author a free hand to devise a route beyond Gisburn in the hope that it would gain official recognition at some future date. She chose to go to the source, the logical conclusion, and gives her reasons for the choice in the next chapter. This development came to the notice of the Yorkshire Dales National Park and the North Yorkshire County Council through whose territories the extension passes, and they both expressed considerable interest. The Countryside Commission provided additional grant aid for this purpose. The Yorkshire Dales National Park undertook to keep an eye on paths subject to additional wear and to signpost the Way wherever it crossed a road.

The entire Ribble Way thus gained official recognition early in 1985.

* * *

THE SOURCE OF THE RIBBLE

A river rarely has just one indisputable source and the selection of one of the many springs that form the headwaters of the Ribble poses questions of geography and history. The Ordnance Survey uses the word 'Ribblehead', implying source to the area where the river becomes known as Thorns Gill. This is too vague to be satisfactory and is at variance with the dictionary definition of the word source. Geographers make their selection by assessing the length and volume of water contributed by various tributaries and the altitude at which they rise.

In the past other writers have made their choice. Let us consider them. At Whitsuntide 1862 William Dobson, who wrote the book 'Rambles by the Ribble' made a little expedition - for that is what it was in those days - to find the source of the Ribble. He claimed it was on Wold Fell. 'There are two springs on Wold Fell and their commingling waters form a tolerable brook when they reach the roadside. The highest of them is only about three to four hundred yards from the highway. We regard it as *the* source of the Ribble'. The highway, he makes clear, is the highest point of the Ingleton-Hawes road. Frederick Riley, writing in 1914 in 'The Ribble from Source to Sea' mentions the geographical desiderata and allows the reader to take his pick. If the name is important, then the source is at Gearstones, if altitude is important, then the source is on Cam Fell, if furthest from the sea, a spring on Wold Fell. Jessica Lofthouse, who was quite a walker in her younger days, discusses the alternatives in her book, 'The Three Rivers' (1949). She considers a spring high on Cam Fell to be one of the 'headsprings' because of its altitude. On the other hand she describes a spring high on Wold Fell as 'the source'. This surely is the same one described by both Dobson and Riley. In more recent times Wainwright in his 'Ribble Sketchbook' pays no heed to geographical niceties. He settles for the roadside junction of Long Gill and Ouster Gill.

The present author feels the need to satisfy geographical constraints more strongly than the need to conform with historical tradition. She has, however, the over-riding requirement to select a spring which can be reached by following a right of way path along the banks of its stream. There is only one candidate: the springs at the head of Jam Syke on Gayle Wold. These springs satisfy the geographical requirement admirably. They are marginally higher than either the Cam End or Wold Fell springs and do not dry up in drought. The highest of them burbles forth in a most satisfying manner from the base of a little limestone cliff. As far as this book is concerned, this spring is *the* source.

THE FAIR FACE OF RIBBLESDALE

For a great many years now Ribblesdale has been dear to the hearts of all Lancastrians who love good countryside. Many are the writers who have described its charms and beauties. This is not a pale imitation of them, but looks at the reasons for the valley's attractiveness.

Rock structures and types are the basis of all scenery, of fundamental importance in assessing the changes that occur in the landscape. Obviously there are big changes in rock types along the length of the valley. All around Preston to just east of the M6 the rock is a warm red sandstone, Buntner Sandstone, for the technically minded. It is exposed by river erosion close to Brockholes and the walker can see how Red Scar Wood gets its name. Beyond this point the rocks are those of the Millstone Grit Series, very much older and harder than the Buntner Sandstones around Preston. Hard rocks tend to give bold features in the landscape and they now appear -Longridge Fell on the north side of the valley, the West Pennine Moors on the south, and continue to Whalley Nab and Pendle Hill. The rocks of the valley floor change again near Dinckley to the Worston Shales. These shales are lime bearing and produce better soils than the gritstones, even though their effect is masked to a considerable extent by a thick layer of boulder clay left by the retreating glaciers of the last Ice Age.

Throughout the length of the river's flood plain, well seen in many places all the way to Sawley, the soils are alluvial, deposits of river silt made by floods over the last few thousand years. These rich soils produce the lush grasses need by today's high yield dairy farming.

Around Clitheroe bands of limestone appear in the landscape, used to build the unmistakable grey-white houses. This is Chatburn limestone, brought to the surface by the faulting which accompanied the raising of the anticlyne on which Clitheroe and this part of the valley stands. It is a much darker limestone than the Great Scar Limestone found beyond Settle.

Clitheroe Castle however is built on a reef knoll, another type of limestone, not so dark and rather friable. There are a whole series of reef knolls running in a north easterly direction through Worston, beyond Skipton into the western edge of Wharfedale. They are thought to be the remains of a coral reef. Chatburn limestone is responsible for the most dramatic feature of the Ribble Way, the gorge between Sawley and Gisburn. Here a wedge of hard Chatburn limestone obtrudes into the Worston Shales, and being so much harder than the shales, has resisted the tendency of the river to wander about and has directed its energies downwards.

Beyond the gorge the Worston Shales ensure that the valley resumes its former characteristics, then near Wigglesworth they give way to Millstone Grits. This is no longer fence and hedgerow country, but stone wall country, for gritstones make good building stone. The South Craven Fault caused the disappearance of these rocks and the appearance of limestone on the surface. It can be seen very clearly at Settle, with Castleberg Hill a white limestone crag perched high above the town. Just north of Stainforth the North Craven Fault brings the extremely old Silurian slates to the surface. These extend to just beyond Horton in Ribblesdale. They are quarried extensively near Helwith Bridge and are easily seen from the Way, particularly if the Moor Head Lane variation is used. Great Scar Limestone lies on top of these rocks and can be seen at the very top of the workings, unquarried.

Just beyond Horton in Ribblesdale the walker has made enough height - and the tilt of the strata favours him - to walk upon the limestone pastures, well drained and giving delightful walking. Here are the caves and potholes of Sell Gill, Calf Holes, Birkwith, all close to the Way. Caves and potholes are a special feature of the Great Scar Limestone, and are formed by water action on the rock. Beyond Nether Lodge the limstone is covered with a thick layer of boulder clay left by the retreating glaciers of the last Ice Age, some 8,000 years ago. For the first time along the route glaciation has played a more important part in the forming of the landscape than rock types. This is partly because the Ribble Valley did not have a large glacier as many of the dales did. The greater flow of ice from the Irish Sea reduced its size, but at the valley head it left its mark in a whole series of drumlins, slightly elongated mounds of glacial debris left by the retreating ice. The Way goes round about and up and down them until it reaches Gearstones. At Thorns Gill, indeed, at the other gills of Ribblesdale, the water has carved through the boulder clay and other debris to reach and cut into the limestone to form a little gorge.

Beyond Thorns Gill the rock strata change to those of the Yoredale Series. These are narrow bands of limestone, sandstone and shale and at this altitude give poorly drained land that will only grow coarse grass and rushes that predominate almost to the very end. Here, as it happens, one of the narrow bands of Yoredale limestone caps Gayle Wold and it produces the verdant greens so different from the rest of the moor. Indeed, it is the junction between this limestone band and the impervious sandstone band below it that causes the springs that are the source of the Ribble.

With such a varied geological background one could expect a wide range of plant species. This is only true up to a point, for there are a number of factors that tend to over ride the effect of differing rock types. These are climate, the covering of boulder clay, the alluvial soils of the river's flood plain and man's many activities - farming, forestry, even walking.

The flowers the walker will see are mainly those of the woodland, the hedgerow, and the wet places, where they are neither grazed nor trampled nor picked. Efficient farming methods mean that all our old meadow land, once rich with flowers, has been ploughed out and the land re-seeded with rye grass and clover mixtures. They are easy to spot - dull deep green fields compared with the paler green of the native hedge banks. Many wet places are in the woodland, for the farmer drains his productive fields, and woodlands, particularly those in deep cut valleys, tend to be left to themselves. One such place is Tun Brook Wood, full of shade and moisture loving plants that thrive in humus rich soils. The vegetation of the Rainber Scar woodland is completely different. Here the rock is Chatburn limestone which produces a soil containing more lime than those derived from gritstones and sandstones, and the commonest tree is the hazel, hardly found in woodland lower down the valley, with a little elm, ash, sycamore and oak. Most of the woodland in the lower valley is a mixture of oak, beech sycamore, elm, hawthorn, and, just occasionally, ash. Again, vast stretches of the Rainber woods support only one or two species of shade loving plants on the ground beneath the trees, for example, wild garlic or dog's mercury, whereas the ground flora of Tun Brook Wood is particularly varied. In Rainber woods there are islands of ungrazed grass which support a rather different collection of plants. There are primroses, great glorious banks of them, patches of speedwell turn the grass blue by the river, and just here and there, the early purple orchid, almost too exotic looking to be true. Long may they remain to give pleasure to the walkers of the Way so, do your bit, look, but do not pick.

The plant population reverts to the norm beyond these woods and not until Upper Ribblesdale is reached will the walker find any marked changes. The reasons are man's grazing animals and the lack of woodland and hedgerows for this is stone wall country. Very occasionally the bird's eye primrose may be found in the wet limestone pastures and the mountain pansy in the uplands above the valley floor. At Nether Lodge the walker leaves the limestone pastures and crosses first the drumlins and then the moors at the foot of the Pennine ridges. Here the underlying rock structures and the boulder clay give badly drained acid soils. There are few flowers to delight the eye: coarse dull green-brown grasses and rushes dominate the landscape, only a stunted hawthorn or two in sight, for here the land is 1000ft and more above sea level, too high for tree growth. Yet at the end, the very end, at the spring that is the source of the Ribble, there is another change. The spring burbles out at the foot of a little limestone crag and here in July the grass is truly green and there are flowers, tiny buttercups, brooklime, scurvy grass, thyme, all in startling contrast with the dull moor around. A fine finish for the botanically minded!

Just as plants are very selective in their habitats, so are birds, largely because of their different food requirements. Birds, like flowers, are seasonal, best seen in springtime unless they are winter migrants. In spring and early summer the most striking bird to be seen on the marshes is the shelduck. It is a large black and white bird with a chestnut band on the chest of the male and flies with the head and tail held low. They are only seen from late winter to early July, for they emigrate after nesting. Though commonest on the mud flats where they feed, the occasional pair may be seen as far inland as Gisburn. Heron may often be seen anywhere along the river, even at Penwortham Bridge, the kingfisher is reputed to be seen from time to time. Water hens and coots may be seen punting along in the quiet pools in many places. Mallard are common enough along the river in springtime, so too, are black headed gulls, oyster catchers and plovers, all looking for nesting sites. In winter Canada Geese arrive to keep the resident gulls company. Small flocks may often be seen on the river where it runs through pasture, for geese are grass eaters.

In springtime on the marshlands the air is vibrant with the song of skylarks, the woodlands resound with the song of small birds. In almost any of them the walker may hear the metallic 'honk-honk' of the pheasant or the gentle cooing of the wood pigeon. More than likely the walker will be surprised by the noisy vigorous flappings of wings from time to time of these self-same birds. Beyond Gisburn there is a subtle change in the countryside. The transition is slow but by degrees the birds of the woodlands disappear and those of the rough pastures and the moorland take their place. There is the curlew with its descending warbling trill, the peewit or lapwing, plovers, occasionally the snipe. These moorland birds preponderate right to the source, but in winter hard weather drives them to the marshes to to find food and they only return in the spring. The arrival of the curlew is a sure sign of the return of spring to the moors.

One could hardly describe the face of Ribblesdale without mentioning salmon: the Ribble has been famous for its salmon for centuries. Fishing rights on the river are controlled by the North West Water Authority and a licence from them is required to fish. Fishing rights are also the property of the landowner and stretches of the river are let out to a number of angling clubs, for salmon is prized as a 'sporting' fish and commands a high price in the market. The salmon has a most unusual life cycle. It hatches in the gravel beds of the upland tributaries in early spring and spends the first three years of its life in the river. On reaching maturity it goes to the sea and after a variable length of time returns in the autumn to spawn. Great numbers of fish swim up the river from the end of September to the beginning of December and this is the best time of year to look out for them wherever there is an obstacle such as a weir or a small waterfall to be passed. Salmon have quite remarklable powers of leaping and swimming up chutes of water. During the time when the fish are 'running' as this annual migration is called, they do not eat, consequently after spawning in January they are very thin and unfit to eat, so this is the close season for salmon fishing. Many of these weakened fish die and may be found on the river banks, partly eaten. This is usually the work of mink, escaped from fur farms, as the otter is now very scarce on the Ribble.

With fertile soils that would bear good crops of corn, a productive river, rich in pastures, sufficient woodland and good building stone it is hardly surprising that in medieval times the lower valley could support a Norman castle, two abbeys and two of their granges as well as a large number of fine halls of residence belonging to the local gentry. Some of these remain today - Samlesbury, Alton, Hothersall, Osbaldeston, Dinckley, Stonyhurst, Little Mitton, Great Mitton, Hacking, Waddow, and Gisburn are probably the best known, and have become part of our architectural heritage. The Industrial Revolution touched Ribblesdale but lightly. The Liverpool to Leeds canal's original route would have brought it into the Ribble Valley near Balderstone and taken it out at Whalley but in fact the canal was built via Blackburn and Burnley. The coal and cotton it brought helped to establish early industry there on a large scale. The railway came rather late into the Ribble Valley - it was 1850 before the Blackburn-Chatburn line was opened by the Lancashire and Yorkshire Railway Company and as it was only a branch line ending at Chatburn it did not bring the good communications that enabled Preston to develop so rapidly. For these two reasons the Ribble Valley escaped the despoilation that the Industrial Revolution brought to so much of the Lancashire countryside.

Above Paythorne the wide marshy expanse of the river flood plain is good for nothing but rough grazing and wild fowl. There was once a proposal to build a reservoir there but nothing came of it. Beyond Settle the river is in an upland environment, Horton-in-Ribblesdale, for example, is 800ft above sea level. Here the climate is appreciably harsher and were it not for the well drained limestone soils the entire valley would be unproductive moorland. In past times its remoteness and climate made life that little bit harder for man and it was never nearly so well populated as the lower valley. Today the lack of woodland, grey stone walls instead of fences and the background of the peaks of Ingleborough and Pen-y-Ghent make a splendid contrast with the lushness of the lower valley.

*   *   *

Ingleborough from the Ribble Way at Gearstones

BEFORE YOU START

In this guide book the Ribble Way has been divided rather arbitarily into sections related to major roads with public transport to help those people who wish to do the Way or part of it as a series of day trips. Cheap accommodation is lacking for most of the Way and camp sites are scarce.

The Paths

During 1984/5 the Lancashire County Council did the work needed to convert a collection of often neglected right of way footpaths and short stretches of road into this new recreational footpath where it lies within the County. In addition a number of new right of way paths were created, some to legalise paths habitually used by the public without that right, others to link or modify existing paths. Improvements were made to a few stretches of path, many stiles were rebuilt, and a new footbridge over the River Calder was built together with many smaller ones over the frequent streams and ditches. Walkers should note that there are many other footpaths particularly by the river. These are anglers' concessionary paths, not rights of way, and although they look attractive, they must not be used. The Way is usually well trodden by the river, but some parts away from it are not at present. Waymarking has been done, but it is rather erratic. Within the Yorkshire Dales National Park the logo will only be found on existing sign posts. There is scope for the walker to use his/her skills interpreting map and guide book.

Maps

The maps included in this book should make the walker independent of any other map purely for route finding purposes. Other maps offer much useful ancilliary information. In the Second Series or Pathfinder maps Sheet SD42/52 covers from Longton almost to Brockholes Bridge and Sheet SD63/73 from here to just beyond Great Mitton. From Great Mitton to Settle only the First Series maps are available at present, (autumn 1984) and these are badly out of date. The 1/25,000 Outdoor and Leisure Map Malham and Upper Wharfedale covers the ground just south of Settle but so little of the route is on it that it is not worth buying for this trip. Its companion map, the Three Peaks, is well worthwhile. A new edition of this map is due in March 1985 and will cover the entire route from Settle to the source.

In the 1/50,000 Series of maps sheets nos. 102, 103 and 98 cover the entire Way. Whilst not so informative as the larger scale maps, they still give a useful picture of the Ribble Valley.

Equipment

No especial clothing or equipment is needed, though it is worth remembering the old couplet:

> Hodder, Calder, Ribble and rain
> All come together in Mitton domaine.

Overtrousers are particularly useful when passing through hayfields after rain. Despite the improvements to drainage and surface of some paths there are still a number of wet places, some caused by springs and streamlets in the woodlands, others, far more obnoxious are caused by cattle churning the ground in wet weather. As the walker must live with these, lightweight boots are recommended as the right footwear in all but the driest weather.

Facilities

A list of facilities available in the towns and villages on or close to the Way is given at the start of each section. Places for refreshment are particularly important as the lower Ribble Valley is a countryside of fences and hedges offering little shelter for lunch breaks in bad weather.

Transport

There is an adequate Ribble bus service for returning to Lancashire from most places as far away as Gisburn, but beyond Gisburn it is considerably more difficult. Here are some details of service numbers as local offices are not always aware of all the possibilities.

There is a good service, Nos. 103, 107, and 108 between Preston and Longton. Longton is also on the TimeSaver routes 723 and 761 and the X27 between Liverpool, Southport and Preston and ending variously in Barnoldswick, Earby and Skipton. People living immediately south of Preston may find it more convenient to finish the first day at Walton-le-Dale, for there they are on a bus route home, than to continue to Brockholes Bridge on the A59. From Walton-le-Dale there is a direct and fairly frequent service to Blackburn and Rochdale. The next bus stop on the Way is at Ribchester, which is served by the No. 11 bus, the Preston-Blackburn service. The bus travels via Longridge and Grimsargh to Preston. Hurst Green and Mitton are served by the No. 9 bus, the Clitheroe-Preston service, every two hours but note that this service does not go via Ribchester. There is no bus service between these two places. Clitheroe town centre is rather off route but this same No. 9 service which starts at Well Terrace can be picked up at Edisford Bridge. A direct return to Balckburn via Whalley by service Nos. 232 or X27 can also be made from Well Terrace which is much closer to

Brungerley Bridge than Edisford Bridge. There is another bus to Blackburn, the 233 which starts at Grindleton and can be picked up at the bridge there. Direct return to Burnley from Clitheroe is not practicable. At Sawley the X27 Earby-Liverpool and the No. 208 Earby to Clitheroe bus stop on the A59 not in the village. Both these buses come through Gisburn stopping at the Ribblesdale Arms. The X27 runs every two hours and goes via Clitheroe, Whalley, Blackburn, Preston, Southport to Liverpool. Running in the reverse direction it will point Yorkshire folk in the homeward direction as it has connections to Skipton by No. 743. This 743 bus runs from Skipton via Burnley and Rawtenstall to Manchester. Pennine Motors share with Ribble Motors a two hourly service, Nos. 580 and 581 between Morecambe, Lancaster and Skipton which calls at Settle and there is an hourly service between Lancaster and Preston, No. 140. Whaites Coaches (Settle 3235/3446) runs a rather infrequent service between Horton and Settle. There is no public transport past Ribblehead.

Clearly all these services may not run indefinitely and the walker must check them. Ring the Ribble Motors enquiry office, Preston 51177. There are two trains each way a day between Leeds and Carlisle that call at Settle. Giggleswick, 1½ miles from Settle is on the Leeds to Morecambe line. Gisburn no longer has a station and Clitheroe's is only open for Dales Rail trains. Without a doubt the easiest and quickest way back to Clitheroe, Blackburn and Preston from Settle and Horton is by Dales Rail excursion train. As the train does not leave until around 7 p.m. it allows the walker to enjoy the whole day whereas return by bus could effectively consume the day. There are, however, some snags. It runs only on the first Saturday of the month, May to October inclusive. It is essential to book in advance using the form on the advertising leaflet available from the stations and Tourist Information Offices. There are no single tickets.

Many people will prefer to use a car for part of their journey and possible parking places are given in the Facts and Facilities sheet at the start of each section. Where bus services are infrequent it can be a useful ploy to leave the car at the end of the day's walk and to take a morning bus to the starting point of the day, but note the lack of buses between Clitheroe and Ribchester.

Accommodation

Walkers are warned that there is no cheap accommodation along the Way until Yorkshire is reached. The first (and last) Youth Hostel is at Stainforth, (on the main road south of the village) and there is a Dales Barn at Horton in Ribblesdale. This is at Dub Cote Farm, a long uphill mile out of Horton on the lower slopes of Pen y Ghent, and is marked on the Three Peaks Outdoor and Leisure Map. Dales Barns are traditional field barns converted into simple but comfortable self-catering accommodation for walkers. Bunks, cooking, washing and drying facilities are provided but a sheet sleeping bag and pillow case are needed. It is necessary to book in advance. Write or ring Mrs J.Glasgow at the farm, Tel: 07296 238. The Dales Barn at Cam Houses is very close to the end of the Way. Write to Mrs S.Middleton, Low Raisgill, Hubberholme, Buckden, Skipton, N.Yorkshire. BD23 5JQ or ring Kettlewell 351. The former Three Peaks Hostel at Gearstones is now closed but the Station Inn at Ribblehead has several bunk rooms. Ring Ingleton 41274.

Otherwise the walker must stay in pubs, farmhouses or guest houses. In Preston there is a cluster of inexpensive hotels on Fishergate Hill, in Stanley Place and Stanley Terrace, all 5 minutes walk from the railway station and the bus stop to Longton, and less than 10 minutes from where the Way enters Broadgate at the bottom of Fishergate Hill. Preston Tourist and Information Office, Town Hall, Lancaster Road, Preston, phone 53731 or 54881 ext. 383 offer a free booklet, 'Where to stay and eat in Preston' that lists them all. The Ribble Way Borough Council, Council Offices, Church Walk, Clitheroe, phone 25566 offer a similiar one that covers the Ribble Valley from Ribchester to Gisburn. Settle Tourist Information Office, Council Offices, Victoria Street, Settle, phone 3617, offer information from Rathmell to Horton in Ribblesdale during the summer. At Horton itself the Pen y Ghent cafe doubles as a Tourist Information Office and will help in finding accommodation. Ring Horton in Ribblesdale 333

Campsites

Campsites are scarce too. There is a caravan site at Ribchester and another at Paythorne that takes tents. There is a good campsite at Edisford Bridge, Clitheroe and that is all the Lancashire part of the Way. In Yorkshire the Langcliffe Place Caravan Site, Settle, takes tents. This is close to the river at Langcliffe. At Knight Stainforth, Little Stainforth, there is a large caravan and camp site with shop and good facilities. The Way passes it. Holm Farm Horton in Ribblesdale, opposite the church, now has a camp site with basic facilities. There are many delightful spots along the Way, but permission to camp must always be sought before actually doing so, and no stream can be regarded as safe to drink.

Last but not least

Some stiles around Helwith Bridge carry a sticker, 'Country land owners welcome careful walkers'. An admirable statement. Careful walkers will always:

1. Take all their rubbish with them.
2. Be careful with matches, cigarettes and stoves.
3. Close all gates, including the difficult ones, so that animals cannot stray.
4. Keep their dog on a lead at all times.
5. Walk in single file in hay fields.
6. Take care not to pollute streams.
7. Enjoy flowers where they are growing.

* * *

EXPLANATION of *Ribble Way*
Large Scale Strip Maps

_____ PUBLIC ROAD
_____ PRIVATE DRIVE OR FARM TRACK
_____ UNFENCED ROAD, TRACK
_____ROAD or TRACK USED BY 🐾
_____ PATH USED BY 🐾
_____ OTHER PATH
_____ BUILDINGS
___ OUTLINE OF TOWN OR VILLAGE
_____ CHURCH, CHAPEL
_____WALL, HEDGE OR FENCE
_____EMBANKMENT
___ESCARPMENT (If space permits)
_____ CAMPING SITE, PUB
_____ RIVER, STREAM
_____ROAD BRIDGE, FOOT BRIDGE
_____ WOODLAND & BUSHES
_____PINES

1 MILE

SCALE OF 10 X 100 METRES = 1 KILOMETRE

The start of the Ribble Way   The Golden Ball, Longton

SECTION 1.
LONGTON TO PENWORTHAM BRIDGE, PRESTON

Facts and facilities at Longton

Mileage: 8.5

Maps: 1/25,000 Second Series Sheet SD42/52 Preston South or 1/50,000 First or Landranger Series Sheet No.102 Preston and Blackpool

Toilets: in a side street almost opposite the Rams Head.

Pubs: the Way starts at the Golden Ball

Cafe/Shops/P.O./Telephone: all in a block of shops opposite the church and close to the Rams Head.

Bus Stop: close to both pubs. The Rams Head is the first one passed when travelling from Preston.

Parking: no public car park. Not possible at the start of Marsh Lane.

The route
The Way starts at the Golden Ball which is at the junction of Marsh Lane and Liverpool Road. Follow Marsh Lane for about a mile to the next pub, the Dolphin, a tiny place known locally as the Fish, and the end of the lane. Go straight ahead over the stile onto the marsh bank.[1]

The transition from the landscape of modern suburbia to the wide skies of the marshes was completed in the last few strides. The scene has gradually become more rural and the landscape noticeably flatter. On the marsh bank you enter another world, a tide-washed world. On a good spring day the air is vibrant with the song of skylarks, no sound of man's works penetrate, all are swept away by the ever present wind. The Ribble is not yet in sight, the narrow slit of river seen over the salt marsh is its final tributary, the Douglas.

Turn right on the marsh bank and walk this boundary between sea and land to Longton Brook. As you approach the obvious bridge keep a look out for a stile through the hedge straight ahead. Then turn left and follow the hedge until it ends in 50 yards or so. Here you will find a stile, the first of a close set pack of them that brings you into the corn field on the edge of the brook. Go through this long field, cross the farm lane and then go the length of another field to rejoin the marsh bank. In due course it makes a big swinging right-hand curve and find yourself on the bank of the Ribble itself.[2,3]

The Preston skyline

If the tide is out you will be surprised at the smallness of the river, a mere streamlet in comparision with the enormous width of the river bed on the bank of which you will walk for the next four miles or so. Preston lies ahead, identifed only by the white needle like spire of St.Walburg's Church.[4] You will gradually zoom in on this in slow, slow motion, until the industrial sprawl blots out the distant view of the Bowlands and the West Pennine Moors, and the spire is framed by a forest of electricity pylons.

In due course cross Mill Brook by a good bridge[5.] Now the wide grassy bank becomes much smaller and there are many little paths. They all go the same way, just take care not to leave the bank.[6] Eventually you will find yourself on a cart-track that leads into the former electricity works, now a scene of industrial decay and the chaos of demolition. Eventually it will be landscaped. The environment improves briefly as you pass beneath the tree clad slopes of Castle Hill, Penwortham,[7] and finally you pass between the river and the allotments to join the A59 at Penwortham Bridge.

Things seen along the Way

1. Longton is a place of fairly ancient origin, though not as old as Preston. It was probably established in the middle of the twelfth century, but today no trace of its ancient origin remains: it is a piece of modern suburbia. The Ribble marshes have been progressively enclosed and the land reclaimed by building earth banks for centuries. The remains of an old bank can be seen running across the fields from the Dolphin to Longton Brook. The one used by the Way was probably built in the 1850's. In the late 1830's the Dolphin was a private house with a garden belonging to a local brewer. It seems reasonable to assume that when the marsh banks were being built the house started to sell beer and became a pub. It is known to have been a pub since 1881.

2. As you are walking the broad bank of the Ribble you will quite frequently see stout posts with chains or cables attached to them. When the port of Preston was in regular use the river had to be kept clear of silt and sand by dredgers. They tied up to these posts whilst

they were working and deposited their loads on the opposite bank forming the huge piles of sand and gravel there.

3.   If you are doing the Way in spring time, you will almost certainly see shelduck in this same part of the Ribble, for its silt beds are their feeding grounds. They are large, quite striking birds, black and white with a chestnut band on the chest of the males, though this can only be seen fairly close to. They fly in a characteristic head and tail down position. After they have nested they emigrate and only return in the spring. With luck you may see cormorants and an occasional heron.

4.   St.Walburg's Church might be thought to be some magnificent medieval building, but in fact was built in 1850-54, the time when Preston's population was increasing rapidly. Its steeple is the top part of a four stage tower and the whole is 300 ft high.

5.   The marshes themselves are almost devoid of flowers, for they are too heavily grazed, but the bridge at Mill Brook cuts them off from the banks beyond and flowering plants are now found. In the wet banks of Mill Brook you will see in early May an uncommon plant called scurvey grass It is not a grass but a remote member of the cabbage family. Further along you may find sweet cicily, a plant common in the Yorkshire Dales, for it likes a limestone soil, and close to the demolition work, giant hogweed abounds.

6.   Oil tanks become sadly prominent on the opposite bank: just past them is the entrance to the Albert Edward Dock, opened in 1892 and now disused and closed with a steel dam. It holds 'The Manxman' the last of the Isle of Man boats and the last steam powered passenger ferry in Europe. It is thought to have been the last boat to sail up the river and can be seen from a distance, though not when you are closer. It is open to visitors and the entrance is on Watery Lane, the A583.

7.   Penwortham was one of the most important towns in Lancashire in Norman times. Nothing remains of it today except the artificial mound of Castle Hill where the motte and bailey castle was built to guard the ford across the river at this point.

*   *   *

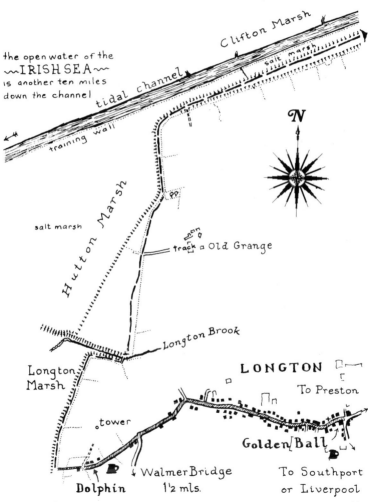

1 MILE

Clifton Marsh

the open water of the
~IRISH SEA~
is another ten miles
down the channel

tidal channel

salt marsh

N

training wall

Hutton Marsh

salt marsh

pp

track □ Old Grange

Longton Brook

Longton Marsh

LONGTON

To Preston

tower

Golden Ball

Dolphin

↓ Walmer Bridge
1½ mls.

To Southport
or Liverpool

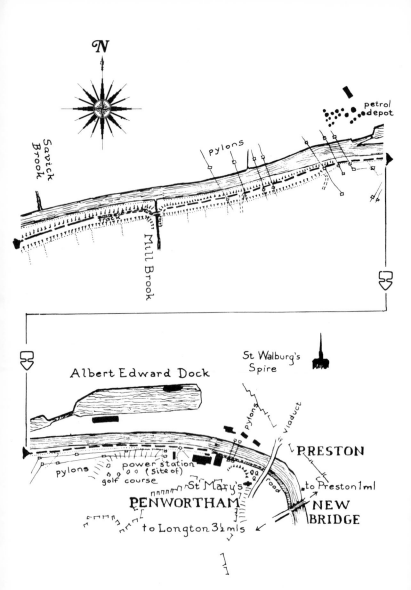

PENWORTHAM BRIDGE TO BROCKHOLES BRIDGE, PRESTON

Facts and facilities

Mileage: 5

Maps: 1/25,000 Pathfinder Series Sheet SD42/52 Preston South
1/50,000 Landranger Series Sheet No.102 Preston and Blackpool

Facilities along the Way

Toilets: in Miller Park on the left after passing under the first railway arch.

Pubs: one at the start of Broadgate, another at the entrance to Miller Park, another at Walton Bridge.

Cafes: chip shop at the start of Broadgate.

Shops: at the start of Broadgate and on Fishergate Hill. Early closing day Thursday.

P.O.: at the start of Broadgate.

Telephone: at the start of Broadgate.

Bus Stop: at the bottom of Fishergate Hill for buses both into Preston and to Longton.

Parking: in Broadgate itself, in the lane by the Shawes Arms at Walton Bridge. Very limited parking in a layby on the south side of Brockholes Bridge. Usually full.

The route

Turn left to cross the bridge and cross the Liverpool-Preston road at the traffic lights - much safer. Broadgate lies straight ahead and you follow this pleasant tree lined street on the very banks of the Ribble[1] until it ends in a gravel road just before the railway arches. Strangely, the scene is almost rural again, quiet, grassy and inviting after the turmoil of Liverpool Road. Purists will obviously start at Longton, but the discerning walker will start at Broadgate. The Way goes under the railway arches[2] to enter Miller Park and follows a pleasant riverside path into Avenham Park[3,4] then into Frenchwood Recreation Ground. It ends in Ashworth Grove, and even there a well situated path follows the river bank right to Walton Bridge[5] on the A6.

A surprisingly good stretch after the poor quality walking before Penwortham. Contrast, presumably enhances enjoyment.

Cross the A6, here dual carriage way and not too difficult, to the Shawes Arms. Go down the right-hand side of the pub and follow the lane until it forks. On the right you will see a stile leading to the riverside path. It gives excellent walking right to the wood.

Here the Ribble slowly meanders across its flood plain between the bluffs on which Higher Walton Church stands and those clothed by Red Scar Woods. You may get your first glimpse of Pendle Hill, which, though it can scarcely be said to dominate the Ribble Valley, occurs time and again in the views. Swallows and martins, quarter the river for midges - and there is often a goodly supply. Black headed gulls and oyster catchers, usually thought of as sea birds, still frequent this stretch of river, for it is tidal almost to Brockholes Bridge but there are too many grazing animals to have a chance of seeing more than the odd daisy until you come to the wood.

The wood contains a number of enticing little paths: all go the same way. Some are wetter than others, take your pick. When you emerge from the wood climb up a little to a higher terrace if need be and follow the path between the golf course fence and the river to the bridge.[7] The Ribble Way now goes under the flood arch to spare you the considerable hazards of crossing the busy road. It appears blocked but there is a stile at the left-hand end and a few yards of newly created path leads you to the farm access road - and to Section 3.

Note

If you want to go into Preston do not use this underpass, but instead follow the path to the left and up to the road, where there is a footpath up Brockholes Brow to the bus stop at the top. If you want to go to Blackburn, use it, for the bus stop is on the far side of the second roundabout.

Things seen on the Way

About Preston

Strictly speaking Preston is only the town on the north side of the Ribble, for that is where it was founded, possibly in the seventh century. Very little is known of that period and not a great deal about the town or village as it was then, in medieval times. However, the structures that may interest walkers of the Ribble Way were all built much later when thanks to the Industrial Revolution, Preston had grown enormously and become an industrial town. It may fairly be said that Richard Arkwright, born in Preston in 1732, was the father of the Industrial Revolution in Lancashire, for in 1770 he invented the spinning or water frame, a machine that, by using

34

The Old Tram Bridge. Winter Hill is seen in the distance.

power from a water wheel, enabled cotton to be spun into yarn far faster than could be done by hand. Arkwright House has been restored and Stoneygate, where it is situated, is easily reached from Avenham Park. Although Arkwright did not exploit his invention in Preston, the town became a major producer of cotton goods and had all the services associated with trade and industry. The following structures passed on the Way are all associated with this period of Preston's history.

1.   Old Penwortham Bridge, Broadgate, was built in 1759, nor was it the first one on that site. The adjacent bridge carrying a collection of pipes once carried the Preston to Southport railway line. The embankment can be seen quite clearly on the other side of the river.

2.   The Preston-Wigan Railway was built in 1838 and the line to East Lancashire in 1850. The two separate railway companies involved built the two bridges in Miller Park.

3.   Avenham Park was established by the Corporation during the period 1861-7 in what had been a market garden area. Avenham Walk, leading to it, had been established as a leisure area and planted with trees as early as 1696.

4.   The Tramway Bridge in Avenham Park is a relic of the heyday of the canal. The Preston-Lancaster canal was opened in 1789 and it was originally intended to connect it to the extension of the Liverpool-Leeds canal at Walton Summit. The problems of crossing the Ribble proved to be insuperable, so a horse drawn tram road was built to link the two together. The first bridge was built of wood in 1802, and the present steel structure in 1860. The tree lined embankment of the tramroad can be seen on the other bank. It was used to take coal from south Lancashire to Preston and places further north and to bring lime to South Lancashire.

5.   There has been a bridge at Walton-le-Dale since 1403. Traces of its embutments can be seen downstream of the present bridge built in 1782 and doubled in width during World War II.

6.   As you are walking along the banks of the Ribble well beyond Higher Walton Church you will notice a solitary brick house across the river. Not far from it the Cuerdale Hoard was discovered by workmen in the banks of the river in 1840. This hoard was a huge collection of around 10,000 early silver coins and a considerable weight of silver ingots. The coins were Scandinavian and were minted between 815 and 930 A.D. It is thought that the Hoard may have belonged to a Danish army as it is too big to have belonged to an individual. It is a matter of conjecture whether the chest was buried whilst the army was in flight or lost in an attempt to cross the river. A

stone marks the site, but there is no public access to it.

7. Brockholes Bridge was rebuilt in 1824 when the Preston-Blackburn turnpike road was being constructed. It is called Halfpenny Bridge locally, for a halfpenny was the cost of the toll. This bridge was swept away by floods in August 1840 and today's bridge built in 1861.

*　*　*

Penwortham Old Bridge

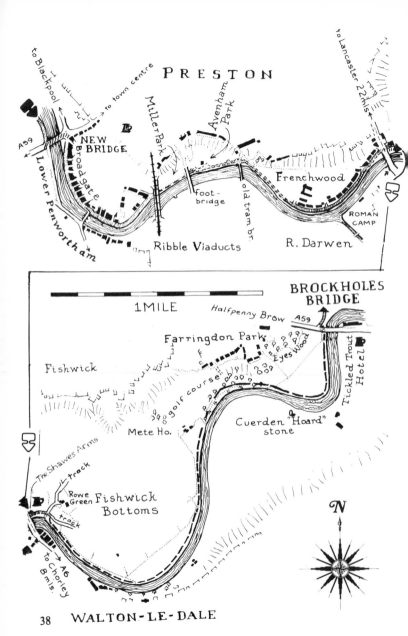

PRESTON

to Blackpool

to town centre

to Lancaster 22 mls.

A59

NEW BRIDGE

Broadgate

Miller Park

Avenham Park

Frenchwood

Lower Penwortham

foot-bridge

old tram br.

ROMAN CAMP

Ribble Viaducts

R. Darwen

1 MILE

BROCKHOLES BRIDGE

Halfpenny Brow

A59

Farringdon Park

Eyes Wood

Fishwick

golf course

Tickled Trout Hotel

Mete Ho.

Cuerden "Hoard" stone

The Shawes Arms

track

Rowe Green

Fishwick Bottoms

track

N

to A6 Chorley 8 mls.

WALTON-LE-DALE

Facts and facilities at Ribchester

Mileage: 9.5

Maps: 1/50,000 First or Landranger Series Sheet No. 102 Preston and Blackpool or 1/25,000 Pathfinder Series Sheet SD63/73 Great Harwood and Longridge.

Toilets: on the car park, well signposted.

Pubs: three

Cafes: tea, cake and ice cream only in summer. Facing the river, passed by the Way. Chip shop in Water Street.

Shops: all kinds on the main street. Early closing day, Wednesday.

P.O.:   in the main street.

Telephone: 100 yards from the P.O.

Car Parking: free car park, well signposted.

The route

When you reach Lower Brockholes Farm, a pleasant building that has evidently seen many alterations and additions, bear right along a wide gravel road. Follow it under the motorway, then take the right-hand fork and follow it past the now demolished Higher Brockholes Hall to where it ends at an iron gate. Go through the gate and turn left up the field into Red Scar Wood. At the top of the woods bear right on a cinder track that runs round the edge of the playing fields. Where it bends left, go into the wood and cross a stile that puts you on a well made path which you follow right to Tun Brook Farm.

Red Scar Wood is a glorious place in springtime before the leaves are fully opened. It is light and airy and from a distance it is seen to be crowned with clouds of flowering cherry. The floor is carpeted with celandine, bluebells and wood anemone: the air is filled with birdsong. There is the occasional metallic 'honk-honk' of the pheasant and the incredibly rapid drumming of the woodpecker may be heard. From the higher part of the path there are tantalising glimpses of the river as it makes a great horseshoe bend below. With regret, this is the last time you will see it for quite a time, for there are no riverside right of way paths until you are approaching Ribchester.

Pass the farm on the left, turn right in the lane, and where it joins another lane in 30 or 40 yds, the stile is straight ahead. Now aim for the opposite right-hand corner of the field to find the next stile. (It can be filthy here from cattle churning the ground.) Then go across

39

the next field bearing slightly right, (a reminder here of the need to walk round unmown hayfields, as this one may be) and look for the stile into Tun Brook Woods[1] supported by steps as it crosses this deep cut valley. When you emerge from the wood make diagonally right to find the stile by the gate into Elston Lane. Turn left and follow this lane for almost a mile, bearing left at the first junction, until you come to a gated lane on the right with a signpost, 'Public footpath to Ribchester via Alston Lane 4 miles'

Tun Brook Wood is substantial enough to act as a barrier to the urban atmosphere - the views of industrial buildings, noise, litter and rubbish around, that marks much of the Way up to this point. Ahead lies the Ribble Valley, rural and unspoilt except for a short stretch around Clitheroe. As you walk along Elston Lane, delightfully quiet, shaded by oak trees and fringed with cow parsley in early summer, you are walking along a shelf on the edge of the valley. The river is down below, making a distant meander. Beyond it you may see the West Pennine Moors identified by Darwen Tower. Great Hill lies to its right, Hoghton Tower is on the nearer wooded hillock that lies between them. Pendle Hill is not yet in sight, only the 'Little End' above Whalley. When you've turned the sharp corner in the lane, part of the Bowlands behind Chipping come into view. Parlick is the lower hill, and behind it, Fairsnape Fell.

Follow this lane through two white iron gates then at the end of the next field look for the stile on the right, for the path goes on the other side of the hedge, still in the same direction. As the hedge swings left keep straight ahead towards the house and you will find the stile on the corner of the field. Straight ahead a stone step stile brings you onto the lane. Turn right and in about 100 yards you will see a sign, 'Footpath to Hothersall Lane'. Though you are indeed going to Hothersall Lane, this is not your way. The Ribble Way takes a far better line. Keep on down the road. In about 200 yards you will see another sign to Hothersall Lane, waymarked to boot, one of the few used on leaving a country lane. Follow the line of electricity poles, keeping about 30 yards to their left to find the way to three partly hidden footbridges. After the last one make your way steeply up the hillside to the right of the wood. Follow the hedge to Stubbins Nook and thence to Hothersall Lane.

Turn right down the lane and follow it down the hill to its end at Hothersall Hall. Go left past the front of the Hall and up the gravel road to where it swings left. Here go over the stile by the gate on the right and aim for the top of the wood and then follow its edge all the way down to the river bank. Again, there have been tantalising glimpses of the river from the road, but here, for a brief spell, you

The White Bull, Ribchester

are close to the river again. After a couple of fields' lengths you reach the rough lane that brings you all the way to Ribchester, passing the Roman Museum and the church on your left. As you stand by the river the school lies straight ahead and the Way goes to its right and by passes the village by a nondescript riverside path to rejoin the main road close to the New Hotel.

It is a pity, though, to miss such a historic and interesting village, the finest visited by the Way. Take an hour or so to wander round it and then make for the New Hotel which is on the Blackburn road at the east end of the village.

Things seen on the Way

1.   If you have an interest in botany and you are doing the Way in spring or early summer, Tun Brook Wood has much of interest. It is sheltered and heavily shaded and having a richer soil than many of the deep cut cloughs of the West Pennine Moors, has a far bigger variety of both trees and herbaceous plants. You will find wych elm, ash, hazel, bird cherry and guelder rose as well as the ubiquitous oak, sycamore and hawthorn. As you descend the east facing side which is

41

wetter than the other, you will find golden saxifrage, yellow pimpernel, ground ivy, herb bennett, violets. I'm sure primroses could be found in some remote corner, for primroses are irresistible and soon plundered. There are two particularly interesting plants, not common in Lancashire: sanicle and our biggest sedge, carex pendula. It grows 3 to 4 feet high, its leaves are blade like, an inch wide, and its flower stalks bear catkin-like heads topped by a thin brownish spike which is the male flower, for sedges bear separate male and female flowers. You may also find this plant in Raisber Wood. At the bottom of the valley there is a path of sweet woodruffe and harts tongue ferns hidden away. The upper part of the opposite side is drier than the rest, parts of it are carpeted with wood anemone, but you will also find celandine, lords and ladies, oxalis, germander speedwell, and dogs's mercury and enchanters' nightshade, two not very interesting plants to look at. The first of them is only found in ancient woodland or hedges that are the remains of woodland. It seems probable that Tun Brook Wood has always been woodland, but this does not mean it has not been cut and replanted many times.

2.   Just before Hothersall Hall comes into sight there is a collection of very modern buildings on the right. This is the Lancashire County Council's Field Studies Centre, where school children do the practical work for their A level geography and botany. Hothersall Hall itself, like all the halls of the Ribble Valley, is on the site of a very much older one. The present structure was built just before World War I, and farms much of the land around. In the fields round here you may see cows wearing collars with coloured plastic boxes. These boxes contain computerised information that controls the amount of supplementary rations fed to each cow according to its milk output. That's modern farming for you!

3.   Osbaldeston Hall is well seen across the river during the last half mile into Ribchester. Like Hacking Hall, still to come, it has a number of gables but it is not so fine. Again, like Hacking Hall - and a great many more houses in the area it was rebuilt in the early part of the seventeenth century and had its own ferry.

4.   Ribchester's attractiveness arises from its rows of neat cottages and houses, relics of the eighteenth and nineteenth century weaving industry rather than from its Roman remains of which disappoint- ingly little can be seen. Some of them lie beneath the churchyard and adjacent houses - part of the rampart can be seen just outside the west gate of the churchyard. After the Roman fort was abandoned it was used as a source of ready cut stone for all sorts of later buildings. The pillars of the porch of the White Bull are reputed to have come

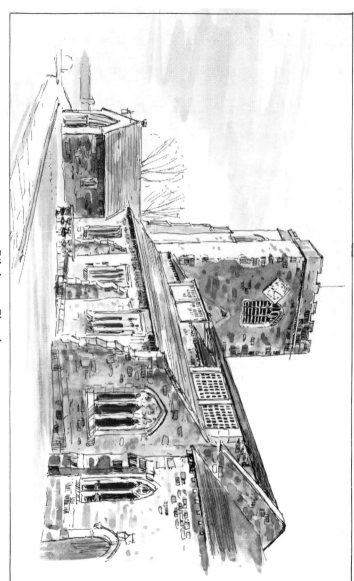

Ribchester Church

43

from the fort, those of the Singing Gallery of the church may have done. The river changed its course in the eighteenth century and washed away the whole of the south east corner of the fort, not a complete loss to archaeology for river erosion uncovered the splendid ceremonial helmet and visor in 1786. It is probably the best of its kind ever discovered in the British Isles. The original is in the British Museum, that in Ribchester is a copy. The fort, Brementennacum, dats from A.D. 79, a time when Agricola was advancing northwards against the Brigantes. It was built to guard the river crossing of the road from Manchester to Carlisle and the road to Ilkley and Kirkham. As it safeguarded such important lines of communication it became one of the biggest in Lancashire and was occupied by heavy cavalry from the Danube. When they retired many of these men settled locally making a large civilian settlement around the fort now covered by the village. The museum has a good display of some of the objects that have been excavated and a painting illustrating how people lived at that time. The excavated remains of the granaries can be seen in its yard, but the only others are the remains of the bath house off Greenside. (From the museum go past the White Bull and turn right into Greenside. Then take the first right and the excavation is at the end of the street.)

The Tower of St.Wilfred's Church beckons the walker as he/she approaches Ribchester. St.Wilfred was Archbishop of York in 664 and a great church builder. This does not imply he built Ribchester Church, but it is quite possible he visited it. The first impression of the building, one of interesting bits and pieces arises because of the many additions and alterations made over the centuries. The main body of the church was built in the early part of the thirteenth century and has a fine triple lancet window characteristic of that period. It almost cetainly incorporates an earlier Norman church -there is a blocked up Norman doorway in the North wall - which in turn replaced an even earlier one. The porch and Dutton choir are fourteenth century work though the fine tower was not built until the fifteenth century. Dutton is one of the townships that make up the parish and the Way goes through it. The church contains many features which will appeal to those interested in church architecture. In particular there are the dormer windows, probably put in about the year 1700 to improve the light in the nave, and the Singing Gallery built in 1736 to accommodate musicians. Under the Commonweath's puritanical administration all church organs had been destroyed and after the Restoration in 1660 simpler musical instruments came into use.

Little or nothing is known of the village during the period of time

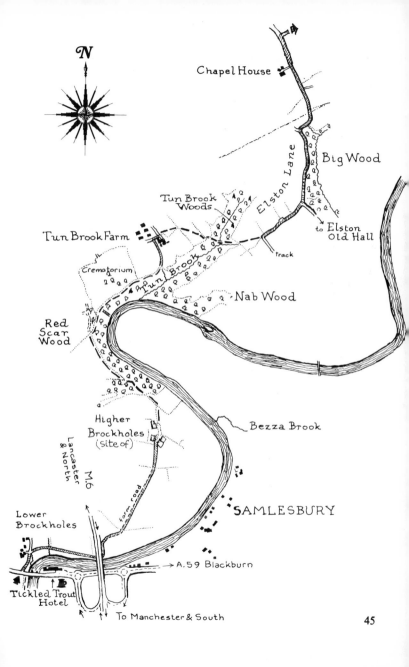

spanned by this church building except that it was pillaged by the Scots in 1332, a not uncommon occurrence in the north of England after the battle of Bannockburn, and that it was scourged by the Black Death in 1349-50. Probably half the population died and it took some 300 years before it returned to its former level. Two or three houses of this period remain, including the White Bull. By 1745 Ribchester must have been enjoying some prosperity, for there is a group of fine Georgian houses, brick built, which is unusual here, but with stone facings. The bulk of the fine stone houses that give Ribchester its character were built somewhat later than that, probably from 1780-1820. Most of them were handloom weavers'houses, for at this time, even until the 1830's, handloom weaving was the minor occupation of the village. It was carried out in the home, sometimes in cellars lighted by two or three windows at pavement level, sometimes in an upper storey or sometimes in a

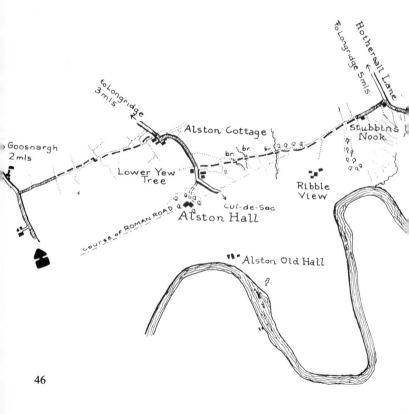

specially built loomshop at the back of the house. The advent of power looms in the 1840s-50s brought hard times and people moved to the nearby towns to find work, even though there were two textile mills in the village. Today Ribchester is partly dormitory village, is partly dependent on engineering, and partly on tourism, for it is a most attractive village in a beautiful valley.

For more information see:

'Ribchester: a short history and guide' by A.C.Hodge and J.F.Ridge.

'A Goodly Heritage' a description of the parish church by J.H.Finch.

The Museum Trust's guide to the Roman period.

These notes are based on the above booklets.

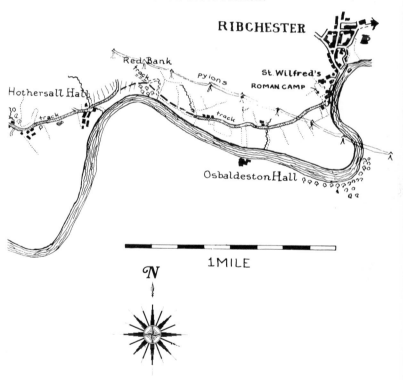

RIBCHESTER TO BRUNGERLEY BRIDGE, CLITHEROE

Facts and facilities
Mileage: 11.2
Maps: 1/25,000 Pathfinder Series SD63/73 Great Harwood and Longridge. 1/50,000 Landranger Series Sheet No. 103 Blackburn and Burnley

Facilities in Great Mitton
Toilets: none.
Pubs: two.
Cafe: by the garage, open all the year round.
Shop: with the cafe.
P.O: none.
Phone: close to the cafe.
Bus stop: at Mitton Road end, a good mile from the cafe.
Car Park: none, but it is possible near the church.

Facilities in Clitheroe
Toilets: at Edisford Bridge, in Brungerley Park, in the market place.
Pubs/Cafes/Shops: Every service in Clitheroe. Early closing day Wednesday. It is 1½ miles from Edisford Bridge, ½ miles from Brungerley Bridge to the town centre.
Bus Station: Well Terrace, but note that walkers who wish to return to Preston are on the bus route at Edisford Bridge.
Car Parking: Car Park and picnic site (not free) at Edisford Bridge. No parking at Brungerley Bridge. Many car parks in Clitheroe.
Campsite: at Edisford Bridge.

The route
This section was walked and described before waymarking was done. There may be a few minor differences between the text and the waymarking. If in doubt, follow the waymarks.

From Ribchester to Dinckley footbridge
Go past the New Hotel towards Stoney Bridge. Before you cross the bridge turn left into the lane that leads to the Roman Catholic Chapel, and after about 50 yards leave it at a stile on the right. Walk the length of this field crossing a little stream by a tiny flag bridge.

There are two stiles ahead. The left-hand one cuts across to the track that leads to Stydd Church[1] an ancient and starkly simple building, and gives a good view of the Stydd Almshouses.[2] It's worth a short diversion. The right-hand stile is the one for the Ribble Way. Beyond it you will find a little bridge. Cross it and follow the hedge to the next field and cross that straight to the road ahead. Turn left along the road and cross the stile on the right immediately in front of the farm ahead. Cut straight down the field to the farm access road by the river, turn left along the access road and follow it to the farm. Here turn right in front of the barn and follow the painted arrows to the riverside, to start a fine stretch of pasture and woodland. Follow the banks of the river pulling away briefly as you approach the wood. There are several paths in the wood, it is probably best to keep near the river until you meet a wire fence, then move left to find the stile. Now you climb quite steeply up the hillside, there is no path at present, but no doubt one will appear with use. Keep towards the left and make for the stile by the gate ahead. Shortly after climb up again to the left to the stile at the side of the right-hand one of two gates. You'll find the next stile in the left-hand corner of the field behind Hayhurst Farm. It puts you onto a farm track, but you cross the stile almost opposite. Pass to the left of the wooden building and follow the hedge to find the bridge. Go straight ahead and follow the hedge through three fields to reach Trough House, with Dinckley footbridge on the right. If you wish to go to Hurst Green or visit Stonyhurst College, see Section 4a at this point.

About ¾ mile downstream from Dinckley footbridge is the whirlpool of Sale Wheel, which spins in flood. The right-of-way path to Sale Wheel passes some of the nicest scenery on the Ribble and is well worth a diversion. Turn right when you have crossed the bridge and follow the riverside path to Sale Wheel, a circular pool past a rocky narrows. Go up towards the road, where the path ends, for the best view of the pool. Then retrace your steps.

From Dinckley footbridge to Great Mitton
Until the Calder footbridge is built the Way continues along this side of the Ribble, the north side, and does not cross the Dinckley foot-bridge. When the bridge is ready, and a date cannot be given at present, the route will cross it and use the south side. Waymarks on the approach to the bridge will show which side to use.

Dinckley footbridge to Great Mitton, north side route
At the approach to the footbridge turn left and go through the farm

Stydd Almshouses

yard of Trough Farm and follow their access road to Hurst Green. Turn right to the Shireburn Arms and right again between the petrol pumps and the bus shelter. At the end of the buildings cross the stile onto a farm road, cross it and continue down the hedge side. Where the fence turns right, cross the little stream by the bridge and continue to follow the stream down the hill. As you approach the wood bear right to find the stile. On the other side of this narrow strip of boggy woodland you will find a well trodden path that takes you across a field then through more woodland very steeply down to a footbridge across Lambing Clough and the banks of the Ribble. Turn left and follow the banks of the Ribble quite closely all the way to its junction with the Hodder near Winckley Hall Farm.

Follow the cart track by the Hodder into the complex of farm buildings. Follow their access road for perhaps ¼ mile, a delightful stretch in springtime with horse chestnuts in bloom. As you approach some brick buildings on the right of the track, look for a hidden swing gate on the right. Now cut across the field to another one near a couple of big trees, then work diagonally right towards the wood.

As you top the rise of the field you will get a view of the cupolas of Stonyhurst College above the trees. They look as if they belong to some foreign land not the Ribble Valley. Wish you had taken the diversion for a better look? All is not lost.

Now follow the wood bearing left at its end to find the stile. The green gate ahead brings you onto the road a good mile from Great Mitton and opposite a lane that will take you to Stonyhurst in about 20 minutes, though it lacks the fine approach given by the route used in Section 4a. Turn right on the road. It has a footpath at first and then a wide grass verge, so is not bad going, but when you reach the first road on the right which is the direct road to Great Mitton, all this changes. This road is narrow and twisting and there are no grass verges. It carries quite a lot of traffic and is potentially dangerous for walkers. Take the greatest care, or if you are not in a hurry, continue for a ¼ mile to the other road (bus stop) to Great Mitton and use that. It is a little longer but much safer. At Great Mitton go past the cafe and garage and over the bridge to the Aspinall Arms where you join the south side route.

Dinckley footbridge to Great Mitton, south side route

Note: The route beyond the Calder footbridge may differ in detail from that given here. Again, follow the waymarks.

Low Hodder Old Bridge

From Dinckley footbridge to Great Mitton

Cross the bridge and turn diagonally left to find the stile, then keep left towards Dinckley Hall Farm.[3] Turn right as you join their access road and follow it up the hill for about 200 yards. Just before you come to a gate - probably open, across the road, - look out for a stile on the left. It's not obvious. Then bear left and follow the edge of the wood to its end, right above Dinckley Hall, then turn right to find the stile a little way up the hedgerow. Keep right to the gate and stile, then turn right and follow the hedge towards the corner, then cut across to the farm on the other side of the field. Go through the little gate by the tree, turn right and almost immediately turn left beyond a large outbuilding and follow the cart-track into the field. When you meet the cross-hedge turn left to find a stile at the barn. From here there is a clear path down to the stream and a little bridge across it. Then a fenced cinder track takes you to the access road leading to Brockhall's[4] market gardening area. Cross the access road and continue alongside the market garden area and a playing field on a well used path. At the next access road go through the gate ahead then at once turn right to find the stile into the upper field. The next stile is now clearly seen and from it make for the left-hand end of the farm buildings. Here go through the gate onto a fenced cart-track which leads you into the field below the wood and onto the river bank again. Turn right and go through the wood and along the pasture to the new footbridge over the Calder, passing Hacking Hall[5] on the right. Then go straight up the field towards the wood, the finest bluebell wood for many a mile. The stile is about 50 yards from the river bank. Follow the path through the wood, then go straight ahead to find the next stile, but to find the one after that, aim at the right-hand field corner. Now go through the green gate ahead and aim for the right-hand side of the farm. Go through the stock yard onto the farm access road but leave it almost at once to walk parallel to the hedge some 50 yards away from the field corner. Here a stile puts you onto the road. Turn left and a couple of minutes down the hill brings you to the Aspinall Arms at Great Mitton. The rest of the hamlet[6] is at the top of the hill.

Great Mitton to Brungerley Bridge

The two routes from Dinckley footbridge arrive at Great Mitton from opposite directions. It you have used the north side route, pass the Aspinall Arms to find the stile. Just before you reach the pub cross the stile on the right and keep on this line to find the other stiles and a footbridge across a small stream. Now aim for the blue-green bridge ahead. Here you will find a stony cart-track leading to a farm, then you follow its access road along the riverside and past Clitheroe's waste disposal centre. Follow the road for about ¼ mile until you have crossed a bridge, then at once turn left on a rough farm access road. It forks in about 100 yards where you will find the stile. Now follow the hedge to the left round two sides of the field, then drop down to the river bank, here badly eroded by flood water. Two fields later you will enter Edisford Bridge[7] Caravan and Campsite. Follow the river bank to the road. Turn right on the road and follow it towards Clitheroe until you come to the public baths in about ¼ mile. Turn left here, and when you've passed the baths cut across the playing fields to the left-hand side of the houses ahead.[8] Keep to the left of them until you see a narrow gravel path on the right. Turn up this then follow the road to the first junction on the left. This will lead you past the disused Wesleyan School[8] to a farm. Go through the gate ahead to enter a straight lane with allotments on the left-hand side. Follow this for about ½ mile when you will see a stile on your left. Now make for the river ahead and you will arrive at or near the weir of the former Low Mill cotton factory.[8] From here there is a delightful riverside path to Brungerley Bridge.[9]

Things seen on the Way
This section of the walk is particularly rich in buildings of historical and architectural interest.

1. Stydd Church.   This chapel is extremely small and simple and has an air of great antiquity. It belonged to a preceptory of the Knights Hospitallers and was built in the twelfth century. The Knights were an order of crusading monks who were dissolved by Henry VIII and their preceptory has long since disappeared.

2. The Stydd almshouses.   This curious Italianate building was erected by one of the Shireburn family in 1728 to house five poor people. There are two dwellings on the ground floor and a wide stone stair case passes between them to reach a loggia with three more dwellings which are sheltered by a three bay arcade of rustic Tuscan columns. They are still in use.

3. Dinckley Hall and ferry.   The white farm building is soon spotted as you approach the footbridge, but its most interesting architectural feature, its cruick built south wall is best seen from the wood above - if there are not too many leaves on the trees. It is known to have been in existence since 1333. Like all the old halls along the Ribble it had its own ferry, which was replaced by the footbridge in October 1951 by the Lancashire County Council.

4. Brockhall is now a hospital for the mentally sub-normal.

Edisford Bridge

5. Hacking Hall. This venerable house is the largest and most elaborate of those close to the Ribble Way. It appears in the Coucher Book of Whalley Abbey of 1374 but the present house was rebuilt in 1607 by Thos Walmsley, then in his 70th year. He lived at Dunkenhalgh near Clayton-le-Woods at the time and built it for his wife so that she could have her own residence after his death. It has been called a house of many gables - there are five under the front roof line. The projecting wings, mullioned windows and massive chimney breast on the south wall give it a most attractive appearance. Naturally it had its own ferry across the Ribble and the Calder and the ferryman lived in the house opposite. This ferry ran until 1954 and was of considerable value to walkers in the area. One of its old boats was discovered in a barn in 1983 and has been restored and is now housed in Clitheroe Castle Museum. This particular boat was about 12ft long and could take 15 passengers, and was in use until 1938 when it was replaced.

6. Great Mitton Church. Though slightly off route the church has such a fine interior it is well worth visiting. It is usually locked during the week though the key may be obtained from the verger, if she is in. She lives in the house at the church gate. The church was built in the late thirteenth century and has had few structural alterations except the Shireburn Chapel, first built about 1440 and rebuilt in 1544 by Sir Richard Shireburn. He died the same year and this splendid chapel houses not only the alabaster effigies of Sir Richard and his wife Maud, but the no less splendid tombs of four more of the Shireburn family. It must be thought strange that the family who lived at Stonyhurst should be buried at Great Mitton Church. It is simply that Stonyhurst, their manor house, was in the parish of Great Mitton, a huge one that extended from Hurst Green to Grirdleton on the north side of the Ribble.

7. Clitheroe's bridges, Edisford, Brungerley, West Bradford and Grindleton are all either used by or are close to the Way. Edisford is by far the oldest, there has been a bridge there since 1339. West Bradford Bridge was built before 1822 but Grindleton was reached by ferry until 1855, and Brungerley Bridge was not built until 1816. Until that date the river was crossed by hipping (stepping) stones.

8. Low Moor Housing Estate. This modern estate, close to Edisford Bridge is on the site of the former Low Moor cotton factory. The factory was started in 1782 and was enlarged by the Garret and Horsefall families after the turn of that century. By 1841 it was a very large spinning and weaving mill with 238 houses and a Sunday School belonging to it. The mill and houses have all been demolished but the Sunday School still stands. The mill was built on

the site to utilise the water power of the Ribble. The river was dammed below Waddow Hall and a leat, still easily visible below the allotments, brought water to the factory. The mill had three water wheels in 1830, later it installed a water turbine, and did not convert to steam until the 1890s. The great pool created by the dam was used as a boating lake in the 1870s.

9. Waddow Hall stands in a fine position above this pool and has belonged to the Girl Guides Association for many years.

Clitheroe

Clitheroe is a market town of considerable antiquity but apart from the Castle Keep and Steward's House has no buildings of special interest. Nevertheless it has an appealing townscape and is well worth an hour or two. The Ribble Valley Borough Council and Clitheroe Civic Society have jointly issued a pamphlet called *'A walk through Clitheroe'* that describes the best features in some detail. The most prominent feature of the town is, of course, the castle built on a limestone reef knoll about 1180 by Robert de Lacy who was Lord of the Honor of Clitheroe. The castle has had many changes of ownership over the centuries but finally both it and the grounds were bought just after the First World War by the residents of the town as a war memorial. The Clitheroe Castle Museum is housed in a fine late eighteenth century house that was built for the Steward of the Honor of Clitheroe, just behind and below the keep of the castle, virtually all that remains today. It is something of a misnomer, for its excellent displays cover most of the lower Ribble Valley. In particular it has a very informative geological display, pre-historical remains and a clog makers workshop in full working order.

Clitheroe

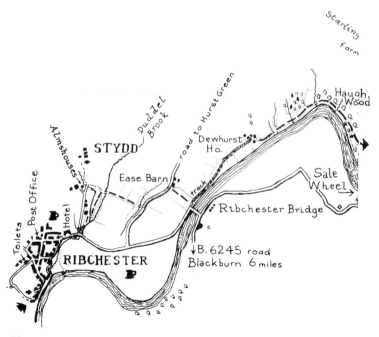

Starling Farm

Haugh Wood

Duddel Brook

STYDD

road to Hurst Green

Dewhurst Ho.

Almshouses

Ease Barn

track

Sale Wheel

Post Office

Hotel

Ribchester Bridge

Toilets

RIBCHESTER

↓B.6245 road
Blackburn 6 miles

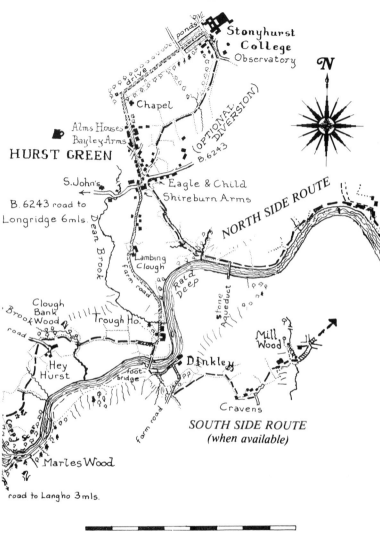

Stonyhurst College
Observatory

ponds

drive

Chapel

Alms Houses
Bayley Arms

HURST GREEN

S. John's

B. 6243 road to
Longridge 6 mls.

(OPTIONAL DIVERSION)
B.6243

Eagle & Child
Shireburn Arms

Dean Brook

NORTH SIDE ROUTE

Lambing
Clough

farm road

Raid Deep

Clough
Bank
Wood

Brook

road

Trough Ho.

Stone Aqueduct

Mill
Wood

Hey
Hurst

foot-
bridge

Dinkley

Cravens

SOUTH SIDE ROUTE
(when available)

farm road

Copp Sc

Marles Wood

road to Langho 3 mls.

N

|◼️◻️◼️◻️◼️◻️◼️◻️◼️◻️◼️|

1 MILE

"The Hodder, Calder, Ribble and rain,
They all meet together in Mitton desmesne."

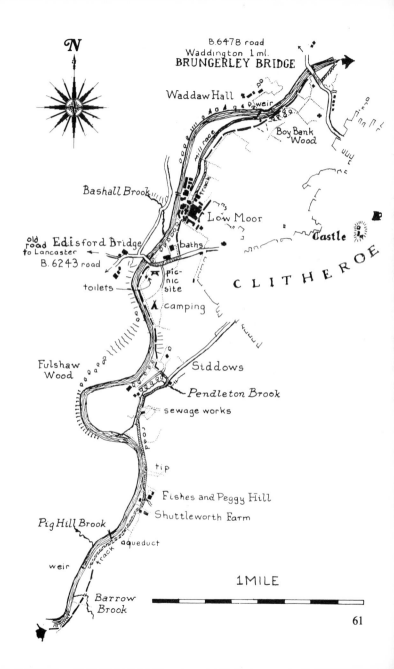

B.6478 road
Waddington 1 ml.
BRUNGERLEY BRIDGE

Waddaw Hall

weir

Boy Bank
Wood

mill race

track

Bashall Brook

Low Moor

old
road Edisford Bridge
to Lancaster ←
B.6243 road

baths

Castle

picnic site

toilets

C L I T H E R O E

camping

Fulshaw
Wood

Siddows

Pendleton Brook

sewage works

road

tip

Fishes and Peggy Hill

Shuttleworth Farm

Pig Hill Brook

aqueduct

weir

track

Barrow
Brook

1 MILE

OPTIONAL DIVERSION TO STONYHURST COLLEGE

Mileage: about ¾ to Hurst Green, a further 2 mile circuit to see Stonyhurst College. Allow about 2 hours for the whole diversion. If you have used the north side route you will find yourself in Hurst Green and an extra hour will suffice.

Facilities in Hurst Green
Toilets: on the right going up Avenue Road.

Pubs: three.

Cafe: on a lane branching off Avenue Road. Can be seen from the Shireburn Arms.

P.O.: with the shop.

Telephone: in Avenue Road.

Bus Stop: close to the P.O.

Car Parking: no public car park. Possible in Avenue Road.

The route
Instead of crossing Dinckley footbridge keep left through the farmyard access road to the public road at Hurst Green. You reach it close to the Shireburn Arms. Go straight ahead up Avenue Road and past the Shireburn Almshouses, now known as Shireburn Cottages. You then enter a short stretch of unfenced road in woodland. Turn right at the end and the classic vista of Stonyhurst at the end of its long avenue of trees, lawns, and lakes lies before you. The building seems distant, but keep going right until you come to the gateway where a notice states that the public are not allowed beyond them. Enjoy the whole placid scene, the stately buildings in their fine setting, the mallard duck, the tame Canada geese, the rare black swan on one of the ornamental ponds.

When you have had your fill, turn right in front of the college. At the end of the buildings the road swings left. Leave it and go through the gate in the corner ahead. Aim for the far end of the wood where you will find the path. Follow the edge of the wood and then the hedge to find a swing gate and then a second one, but at the third turn left just BEFORE it. Now follow the hedge until it meets a wall, where you turn left and walk alongside to a short lane that will bring you into Avenue Road. Return as you came to Dinckley footbridge.

Stonyhurst College
The college is a well known Roman Catholic public school and has been at Stonyhurst since 1794. The College was founded in France in

Stonyhurst College

Henry VIII's time in order to offer English catholics the type of education denied them by him. During the French Revolution it was experiencing problems in France so the Weld family of Dorset (who inherited the Stonyhurst property) offered it to the school, who had just lost their own house. Stonyhurst has a very long history. The house was the manor house of the Shireburn family for at least 400 years until the line died out. Sir Richard Shireburn began to build a new house in 1592 and the present Gatehouse is part of it. It can be seen quite well from the gateway marking the limit of public access. Generations of the family continued to live there, each making additions or alterations until the family died out in 1717 with the death of Sir Nicolas Shireburn. He was the man who built the two big cupolas, a landmark for miles around. He also laid out the grounds afresh making the avenue approach used in this book. Obviously the new owners of Stonyhurst started a repair and rebuilding programme to suit their needs, in particular the church between 1832 and 1835. In the mid-nineteenth century there was a boom in public school building and the next 40 years saw the main buildings as we see them today completed. The school houses a museum which contains priceless relics of Renaissance times and a library with some very rare books.

The Shireburns did not expend their entire wealth on their house at Stonyhurst. Like most wealthy families of the period they were concerned for the welfare of the poor and built the almshouses at Hurst Green in 1707. Originally they were on Kemple End, Longridge Fell and were moved from that unsuitable site and rebuilt in Hurst Green in 1946. The Shireburns, you may remember, built the alms houses near Ribchester. They built the village school in Hurst Green in 1686 but little of this building is left. Earlier members of the family built the Shireburn Chapel at Mitton Church, but some of the later clung to the old faith after the Reformation and suffered loss of lands and property as a result.

*   *   *

SECTION 5
BRUNGERLEY BRIDGE, CLITHEROE, TO GISBURN

Facts and facilities
Mileage: 10.5
Map: 1/50,000 Landranger series Sheet 103 Blackburn and Burnley

Facilities at Sawley
Toilets/cafes/shops: none.
Pubs: one, passed on the Way.
Telephone: on the road that leads to the A59.
Bus Stop: on the A59.
Parking: roadside by the river.

Facilities at Gisburn
Toilets: Close to the junction of the A59 and the Bolton by Bowland road.
Pubs: three in the main street.
Cafes: several.
Shops: in the main street.
P.O.: opposite the Ribblesdale Arms.
Telephone: on the Skipton side of the church.
Bus Stop: in the main street near the Ribblesdale Arms.
Parking: no car park. Room for a few cars near the toilets.

The route
Brungerley Bridge to Sawley
Turn right on the road and in about 100 yards you will come to the entrance to Brungerley Park (toilets). Stay on the lowest path in the park until a waymarked path leaves it on the left to follow the river through fields. Now follow the river bank right to the road at West Bradford.

Here you are directly below the Ribblesdale Cement Works whose chimneys can be seen from many a mile away belching steam and smoke and whose rumblings and growlings bring back the industrial atmosphere of Preston to an otherwise charming bit of riverside. Noise is indeed a pollutant.

Cross the road and continue to follow the river bank until the river starts to swing away to the left. Here you climb up a little and then follow a track between trees to the road between Chatburn and

Grindleton. There are fine views of Pendle, standing grandly above the chimneys of Chatburn, and others up the river to Sawley. Turn left along the road and cross the bridge. At once turn right into the field at the sign post 'Footpath to Rathmell Syke' and follow the flood bank of the river past the confluence of Swan Brook. Then look for a stile in the hedge, turn right and when you meet the little brook turn left and follow it to the stile. Now go straight ahead up the hill for two field lengths to find the stile onto the road. Turn right and follow the road for about a mile to the Spread Eagle Hotel. Cut the corner to the bridge by going through a stile on the right opposite a row of cottages.

Sawley to Gisburn

Bear left at the pub and where the road swings right up the hill keep straight ahead through the ornamental stone gateway onto the private road to Sawley Lodge. As you approach a similar gateway turn left through a farm gate into a field. After about 100 yards turn left across a bridge over a ditch into the field. Turn right and follow a line of stiles until you meet the river bank again at the entrance to Rainsber Wood. (Note. This section, some of it a diverted right-of-way path, is very well waymarked.)

You are now starting the finest part of the Ribble Way. Sometimes the path goes close to the river bank, sometimes it climbs quite steeply above it through the woods, sometimes through islands of pasture. Always it is utterly unspoilt, peaceful, serene, as the river flows in a deep cut valley remote from the rest of the world. On a fine spring morning you may see the fish rising to fly, watch a water hen shepherd her brood of coal black babies around the shallow margins, or be aroused from your daydreams by the quack-quack of a pair of mallards. Take care you do nothing to mar this marvellous bit of riverside.

Continue through this paradise until you have crossed a ladder stile, the first since entering the wood. Now bear right up hill, slightly away from the river. At first you follow a grassy bank which develops into a cart-track. When the cart-track ends you are on a grassy terrace above the river. Keep along it to find the stile on the right. Go up the field to cross the deep cut rivulet then return left and follow the fence to the top side of a barn where you will find a stile. Now turn left and follow the wall to the farm access road. Turn right and just before you reach a group of buildings, turn left through a not very obvious stile. Continue straight ahead aiming for a gap in a belt of woodland. As you emerge from the wood keep straight ahead to find the stile to the left of the cottages. Turn right on the road,

Sawley

then left and left again when you reach the public road. (Unless you wish to visit Gisburn, which lies 10 minutes walk along this road to the right.)

Things seen on the Way
Sawley Abbey
Sawley Abbey is quite often known as Salley Abbey, its original name. Like Whalley Abbey it was a Cistercian foundation and one could expect it to have been a daughter house of Whalley. This was not so. It was a daughter house of Fountains Abbey which owned a great deal of land in the Yorkshire Dales. It was founded in 1147, whereas Whalley was not established until 1216, rather late, because it had been at Stanlow, Cheshire in its early years. The gaunt ruins of the Abbey are easily seen from the road corner by the Spread Eagle Hotel and though at first sight there is little left above ground there are surprisingly extensive foundations, laid bare by the Ministry of Works. The Abbey was never wealthy like its parent house. Its lands were poor and the climate harsh and this is reflected in the quality of the stonework. There is very little ashlar masonry and large parts of the walls are simply built of crude stone blocks, some of it the very easily weathered Worston Shales, the cause of the gaunt and decrepit appearance of the remains. After the Dissolution of the Monasteries in 1536 much of the better stone was carted away and re-used. This was a common practice. Still worth a visit and entry is free.

Rainsber Scar
Rainsber Scar, the crag in the curve of the river, is the scene of Sir William Pudsay's leap. He was a coiner in the sixteenth century who made his own money from silver obtained from a mine on his own estate at Rimington. On discovery he fled from justice and it is said that to escape his pursuers he and his horse leapt the Ribble by jumping down the Scar. He was uninjured, made his escape and was eventually pardoned by Queen Elizabeth I.

Gisburn
Gisburn is a pleasant open village but lacks any buildings of note. Even the church, though superficially attractive hasn't got the interesting features of Mitton or Ribchester. The village's main claim to modest fame is that Gisburn Hall has been the home of the Lister family for almost 200 years. The Listers became Lords of Ribblesdale in 1797 and the first lord is said to have planted more than a million oak trees on his property, and a later one saw to it that the railway line, built in the 1880s, went through a tunnel where it passed close to the house and park.

A corner of the ruins at Sawley Abbey

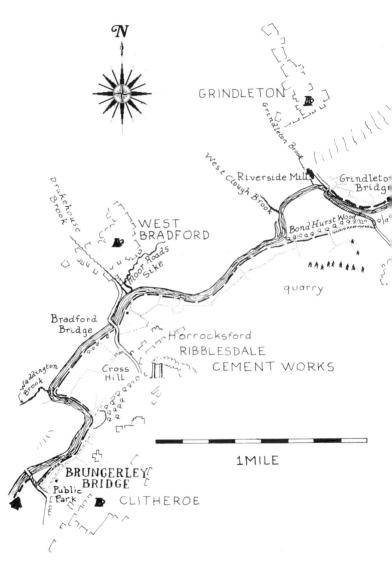

N

GRINDLETON

Grindleton Brook

West Clough Brook

Riverside Mills

Grindleton Bridge

Drakehouse Brook

WEST BRADFORD

Bond Hurst Wood

Moor Roads Sike

quarry

Bradford Bridge

Horrocksford

RIBBLESDALE CEMENT WORKS

Waddington Brook

Cross Hill

1 MILE

BRUNGERLEY BRIDGE

Public Park

CLITHEROE

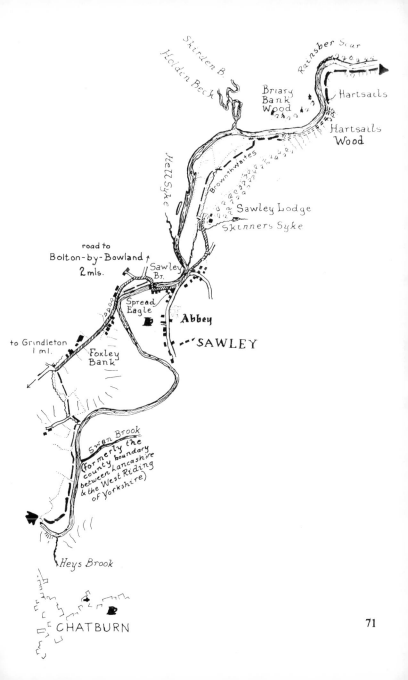

Skirden B.

Holden Beck

Rainsber Scar

Briary
Bank
Wood

Hartsails

Hartsails
Wood

Hell Syke

Brownthwates

Sawley Lodge

Skinners Syke

road to
Bolton-by-Bowland ↑
2 mls.

Sawley
Br.

Spread
Eagle

Abbey

- - - **SAWLEY**

to Grindleton
1 ml.

Foxley
Bank

Swan Brook
(formerly the
county boundary
between Lancashire
& the West Riding
of Yorkshire)

Heys Brook

CHATBURN

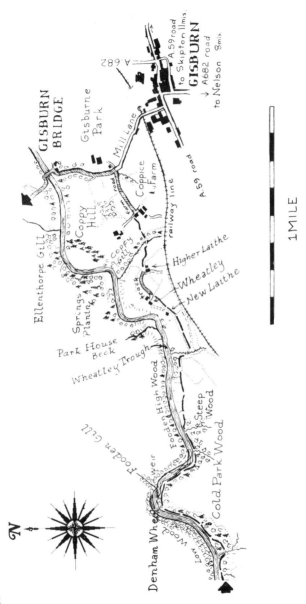

GISBURN BRIDGE

Gisburne Park

Ellenthorpe Gill

Coppy Hill

Springs Plantn

Park House Beck

Wheatley Trough

Fooden Gill

Denham Wheel

Low Wood

Fooden High Wood

Steep Wood

Cold Park Wood

Mill Lane

Coppice Farm

Coppy Gill

railway line

Higher Laithe

Wheatley

New Laithe

A.682

A.59 road
to Skipton 11 mis

GISBURN

A682 road
to Nelson 8 mis

A.59 road

weir

N

1 MILE

72

Facts and Facilities

Mileage: 10

Maps: 1/50,000 Landranger Series Sheet 103 Blackburn and Burnley. 1/50,000 First Series Sheet 98 Wensleydale and Wharfedale. 1/25,000 Outdoor Leisure Series Malham and Upper Wharfedale, but see note in page 20. 1/25,000 First Series.Hellifield. Sheet 85.

Facilities in Paythorne

Pubs: the Way passes it.

Phone: opposite the pub.

Campsite: visible from the Way. Turn left on the road to find it. No other facilities, but obviously, no parking problem.

Facilities in Halton West

Shop and P.O.: Keep right on the road, ¼ mile.

Facilities in Rathmell

Shop and P.O.: near the church.

Phone: opposite the church.

No other facilities.

Facilities in Settle

Toilets: in the car park close to the railway bridge on the A65 and under the Council Offices in the main street.

Pubs/Cafes/Shops: plenty of these in Settle. Early closing day: Wednesday.

P.O.: at the back of the Council Offices.

Bus Stop: opposite the Council Offices.

Parking: see toilets, also in the Market Place.

Campsite: at Langcliffe Place, about ½ mile out of Settle off the Stainforth road.

A Note about the Way from Gisburn to Settle

This section of the Way received official recognition much later than the previous ones and neither work to upgrade it nor waymarking had been done when the author check-walked it in May 1985. Although this section uses right-of-way paths or roads throughout, a number of diversions to sections of path are being processed. These are either to avoid farm stock yards or permanent hay meadows and the Way will be the better for them. It is not known whether field work will be completed before the publication of this guide which describes the route from Gisburn to Rathmell as you can expect to find it when work is complete. From Rathmell to Settle, with one exception, there is no path diversion work in hand at present and the Way is described as it is. Many of these paths have had little use in recent years and there are few 'beaten trods' to follow. Route finding demands considerable care until waymarking has been done. Then follow the way marks, even if they are not in complete agreement with the text.

The route
Gisburn to Paythorne
When you reach the Bolton-by-Bowland road at Gisburn turn left (unless you wish to visit the village) and follow it across the Ribble to the first lane on the right, about ½ mile.[1] Follow this lane and in a short half mile take the farm road on the right. Follow it to its end at Windy Pike Farm. Now turn right through a gate onto a stony cart-track which will bring you to Moor House Farm. As you approach it you will come to a rough cross roads. Hereabouts look carefully for way markers as there may be a right-of-way path diversion away from the farm at this point. However, the present right-of-way path is as follows: go straight ahead to the left-hand side of the house ahead, turn to the right behind it, and go through two gates in quick succession into the field. Go straight ahead to find the bridge over the stream and continue in this general direction aiming at a pine tree with a broken top. You will find three stiles in line then you will be opposite the Paythorne Caravan Site.

Aim at its right-hand corner and when you come to a surprisingly deep-cut stream turn right and drop down to it to find a wooden foot-bridge about 100 yards lower down. On the other side of the little valley bear diagonally right until you come to the hedge, then turn left and follow it to the gate. Here turn left on the cart-track for a short distance in order to cross the stream, then go up the field bearing right a little to follow the power lines to the stile besides the pub, the Palmers Arms.[2]

Paythorne to Halton West
Note that the route over Paythorne Moor is particularly difficult to find at present.

Almost opposite the pub is the bridleway to Nappa Flats, a good farm access road. Go along it for about 10 minutes and when you come to a cattle grid by a solitary barn, turn left into a grass lane between earth banks, much overgrown and not obvious at present. Follow this until it becomes a gravel cart-track, then at once turn right and follow the hedge, go through a gate into another green lane between low banks, often very wet. It is much better to walk on its right-hand bank. Follow this until it ends rather abruptly by a ditch and a fence. Cross the stile and aim for the end of the hawthorn trees on the left to find the next stile. You can see Halton West, and now the difficulties start. Aim for the right-hand end of the hamlet and you should find yourself crossing a raised bank, once a hedgerow, close to a big ditch. Cross the ditch as soon as you can and then aim for a group of small trees bent to the right by the wind, for here you will find the bridge. Now go through the gate in the wall and keeping 30-40 yards from the hedge, walk parallel to it until you cross the small stream. Now aim direct for the green painted barn to find the gate in the corner of the field, not easily seen. Go straight ahead to the road.

Halton West to Cow Bridge, Long Preston

Turn right and 50 yards away you will see a fingerpost 'Bridleway to Deep Dale'. Turn up this lane and follow it to Low Scale Farm. As you approach the farm look for a sign diverting you to the left to go round the farmyard. You will rejoin the main track just beyond the farm. Continue along the farm track until you are almost at the barn, then turn left into the field and pass behind it. Go through the gate ahead and follow the stream. Immediately after the next gate, which is a little snicket gate, turn right and go over the stile in the hedgerow ahead. Now turn left and follow the hedge then make for the gate in the middle of the next fence. Now aim for the gate next to the wood where you rejoin the farm access road and follow it to Cow Bridge.

Though tarmac, this is no bad thing for a while. The mind can relax and enjoy the scene. The hills behind Long Preston are just coming into view and one can detect with some satisfaction the long hollow in which the Ribble runs. It has been so long out of sight it might well be out of mind. In springtime the banks of the lane are a delight, thick with primroses. I beg of you not to pick them but leave them for others to enjoy.

Cow Bridge to Rathmell

Follow the well marked path from the fingerpost 'To Rathmell' along the banks of the Ribble, at last regained, then to the left along Wigglesworth Beck. You will join a gravel farm track just before Wigglesworth Hall Farm. Go straight ahead on it, bear right through the gate, cross the bridge and then turn left onto the farm's access road. As soon as you have crossed the cattle grid turn right, leap the little stream and climb up left of the farm buildings and go through the gate ahead. Now pass by the electricity supply pole and drop

75

Monastic remains at Wigglesworth Hall Farm

down to rejoin the main farm cart-track. Follow this until it starts to climb away to the left towards a couple of trees. Here you go almost straight ahead to a stile that is out of sight. Go straight across the field below the wall to a corner on the left, cross an extremely narrow field and then climb up towards the wood. At the wood turn right and you will find a new bridge over the stream. On the other side

Rathmell - the Reading Room and War Memorial

turn right at the new post and wire fence and follow it to a gate on to the road.

Rathmell to Settle
Walk along the road right through the village. Take great care. Walk in single file and face the traffic, the road is quite busy at weekends. Beyond the village at the bottom of the hill there is a layby on the left. From it a new path will go through the fields to the access road to Hollin Hall. If it is waymarked, use it, if not stay on the road until you come to fingerpost and stile marked Settle. The new path will bring you opposite this fingerpost. Here bear left to find a flag bridge to the right of a solitary hawthorn tree. You need that bridge. Then make for a short length of wall in a hedgerow to find the next stile. From it you can see the Ribble again. Make for it, go under the railway bridge and follow it almost into Settle.

This is a delightful stretch of river - close cropped turf, a fine line of mature beech trees probably planted 130 years ago by the owners of Anley House, the fine house visible from the road. All, of course, provided you keep your eyes turned right. The leftwards and forward views are not attractive.

As you are approaching the road the river swings right, but you keep straight ahead to a little swing gate onto the road. If you want

Approaching Settle

to visit Settle turn right on the road and follow it to the town centre in about 10 minutes. Otherwise go straight across the road into a short street of new houses and bungalows. At the far right-hand corner a right-of-way path goes between them to a little gate leading into a rugby field. It leaves this for the riverside by a small gate on the right, and when you leave this field, avoid the rather obvious cart-track on the left, it goes to Giggleswick. Stay on the river bank path right to Settle Bridge on the A65. If you have been into Settle[3] already, pick up the Way at this point.

Things seen along the Way
1. Ellenthorpe Farm at the road junction keeps the kennels of the Pendle Forest Fox Hounds.

2. Paythorne is one of the very few villages in North Lancashire that is mentioned in Domesday book (AD 1086). Castle Haugh, close to the main road, A682, is almost certainly the site of an early Norman motte and bailey castle, built of wood, not stone. Perhaps Paythorne's greatest claim to local fame is Salmon Sunday, the third in November, when crowds of people from East Lancashire used to gather to watch the annual 'running' of the salmon to their spawning beds high up the river. Pollution mainly from the Calder and Darwen became so great in the post war years that the salmon no longer came in quantity, but now pollution has been reduced sufficiently to allow them to run again in numbers. If the time of year is right and you want to have a look, turn right on the road by the pub and follow it to the river bridge.

3. Settle is another place of ancient origin with a satisfying 'higgledy-piggledy' market place. This is not the oldest part of the town which lies in the steep lanes of Upper Settle. The Craven Museum is on one of these, Victoria Street, and has some items from the building of the Settle-Carlisle railway. The Way goes along the river bank giving a good view of a one time water powered cotton mill, now used for farm storage. It took its water from the weir whose remains can be seen just below the bridge on the A65. At the other end of this bridge there is another former cotton mill whose weir and water wheel are still there. Langcliffe Mill, well seen on the next section of the Way is another of these early mills. They seem a long way indeed from Preston and its cotton mills, and the reason for their establishment was two fold: the availability of abundant water power and the arrival of the Liverpool to Leeds canal at Gargrave in the early years of the nineteenth century enabling cotton to reach the water power much more cheaply.

* * *

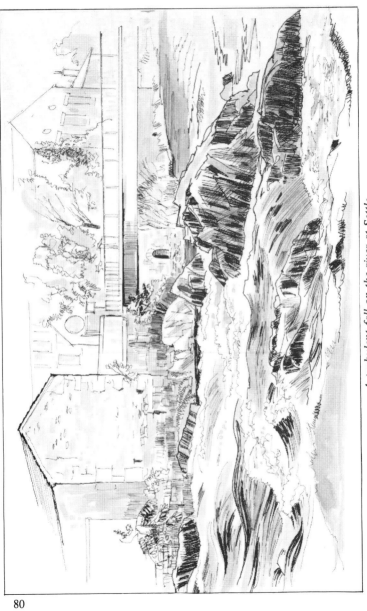

A turbulent fall on the river at Settle

1 MILE

N

Carholme Beck

Settle Lane

Ing Lane

track

Palmers Arms

Paa Lane

barn

Dodgson Gill

PAYTHORNE

Twin Gills

track

Neps Lane

road to West Marton

PAYTHORNE BRIDGE

6 mls

Moor House Farm

cart track

Castle Haugh

Windy Pike farm

farm road

Carters Lane

Tumulus

Ellenthorpe

Stock Beck

GISBURN BRIDGE

road to Gisburn 1 mile

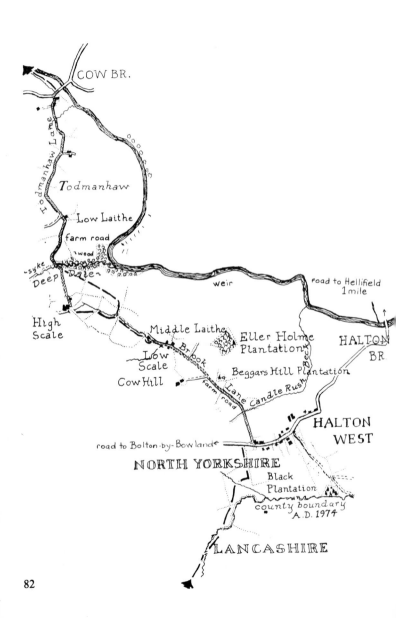

COW BR.

Todmanhaw Lane

Todmanhaw

Low Laithe

farm road

wood

syke

Deep Dale

weir

road to Hellifield
1 mile

High
Scale

Middle Laithe

Eller Holme
Plantation

Brook

Beck

HALTON
BR.

Low
Scale

Cow Hill

farm road

Lane

Candle Rush

Beggars Hill Plantation

HALTON
WEST

road to Bolton-by-Bowland

NORTH YORKSHIRE

Black
Plantation

county boundary
A.D. 1974

LANCASHIRE

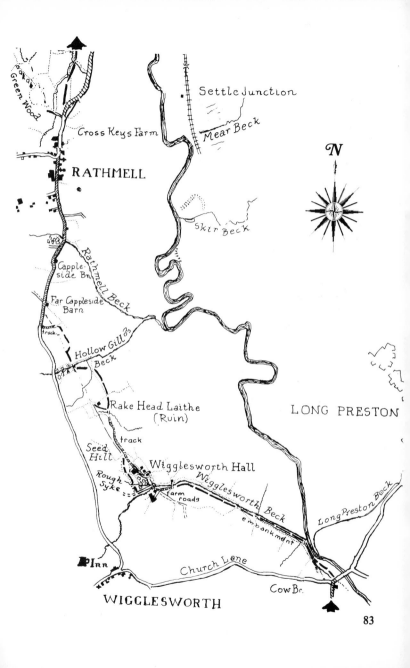

Green Wood

Cross Keys Farm

Settle Junction

Mear Beck

RATHMELL

N

Skir Beck

Rathmell Beck

Capple-
side Br.

Far Cappleside
Barn

Hollow Gill
Beck

track

LONG PRESTON

Rake Head Laithe
(Ruin)

track

Seed
Hill

Wigglesworth Hall

Rough
Syke

Wigglesworth Beck

farm
roads

Long Preston Beck

embankment

Church Lane

Inn

Cow Br.

WIGGLESWORTH

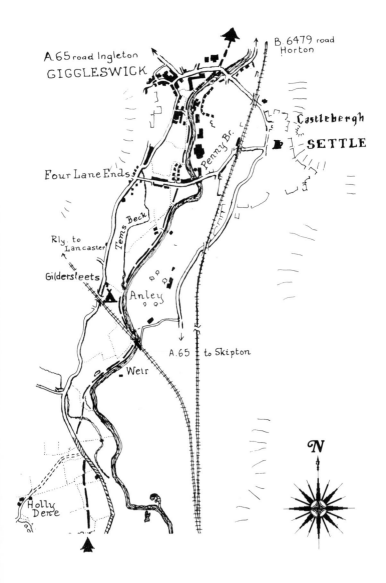

A.65 road Ingleton
GIGGLESWICK

B. 6479 road
Horton

Castlebergh

SETTLE

Penny Br.

Four Lane Ends

Tems Beck

Rly. to
Lancaster

Gildersleets

Anley

A.65 to Skipton

Weir

Holly
Dene

N

SECTION 7
SETTLE TO HORTON IN RIBBLESDALE

Facts and facilities
Mileage: 7 or 8 depending on the route.

Maps: 1/25,000 Outdoor Leisure Maps, Malham and Upper Wharfedale and The Three Peaks. See note on page 20.

Facilities at Stainforth
Toilets: in the car park on the bypass.

Pubs: one in the village.

Cafe: in the village opposite the pub.

Shop: in the village opposite the pub.

P.O.: on the road leading to Goat Scar Lane.

Telephone: at the back of village, signposted by the shop.

Bus Stop: by the pub.

Parking: see toilets.

Facilities at Horton in Ribblesdale
Toilets: in the car park near the river bridge.

Pubs: one.

Cafe: the well known Pen y Ghent Cafe, a mecca for all walkers, on the main road just south of the car park.

Shop: with the Post Office.

P.O.: close to the Pennine Way path to Pen y Ghent.

Telephone: between the cafe and the car park.

Bus Stop: opposite the cafe.

Parking: see toilets.

Note
At present there is no right-of-way path along the river between Little Stainforth and Helwith Bridge, and you must follow the minor road. If, however, you wish to go into Stainforth itself, the alternative via Moor Head Lane is worth considering, but it makes a lot of height for nothing and you come down the lane staring at the quarries of Helwith Bridge.

The route
The signposted path to Stackhouse starts across the road. Follow it round the edge of the Settle School's playing fields to a stone step stile then through fields above the river to the road. It is well used

Langcliffe Mill

and has fine views across the river to Pen y Ghent.[i] Turn right on the road and follow it for a few hundred yards until you come to a white house on the right. Turn right here and follow a narrow lane to the river. The weir and salmon ladder are worth a moment, then turn left and follow the river banks all the way to the old pack horse bridge at Little Stainforth. This is a very fine stretch of river scenery with a splendid climax of deep pools and a waterfall just below the pack horse bridge. The path is well marked most of the way. When you are approaching the caravan site go over the ladder stile to the river bank and follow it to the bridge. Here, if you want to visit Stainforth,[2] turn right on the road and right again in the bypass, then first left into the village. It is a good ten minutes walk. Otherwise, turn left at the bridge, then right on the minor road ahead. Follow this until the wall ends where you will find a cart-track that enables you to cut the corner to the Austwick - Helwith Bridge road just outside Helwith Bridge.[3] Turn right here and after about ¼ mile turn left up the lane by the side of the former village school. After about ½ mile go under the railway bridge into a short lane and follow it past a footbridge (which only goes to the road.) This lane becomes very wet or even waterlogged in parts until it ends rather vaguely in a field. Now go slightly left towards a big bend in the river as you approach Crag Hill Farm. Keep close to the river at the farm and follow the river bank all the way to the Crown at Horton in Ribblesdale. Turn right to find the facilities. This is not a right-of-way path at present, despite it being shown as such on the 1/25,000 map. However, it has been well used for many years and the Yorkshire Dales National Park have work in hand to rectify the situation. Turn right to find the facilities.

Alternatives from Stainforth via Moor Head Lane

Continue past the car park, turn left at the road junction, and go along a narrow lane between the houses at the point where the road turns right. You will see a finger post to Moor Head Lane. Once in the field strike diagonally right steeply up the hill to the wall corner. Then follow the little beck for a while until you can see a ladder stile ahead. Now keep in this general straight line through large fields of rough pasture until you reach Moor Head Lane. Turn left and follow it to the road. Turn left here and right at the junction ahead to reach Helwith Bridge and join the main route at the former village school ahead.

Things seen on the Way
1.   The mill by the river so well seen from the footpath just past the

The old packhorse bridge and Stainforth Force

playing fields is another relic of the Industrial Revolution around Settle. It is one of the oldest and took its water supply from the weir and mill pond at Langcliffe.

2.   Stainforth has some picturesque corners including stepping-stones across Stainforth Beck, whereas Horton has lost all its charm in Victorian villas, railway cottages and modern bungalows. Its church makes up for it: a fine building retaining some of its early Norman work, for it was sensitively restored in Victorian times, whereas Stainforth's was virtually rebuilt.

3.   If you are interested in geology take a closer look at the quarrying at Helwith Bridge. Exactly what you see depends on the current state of quarrying. Two things are clear: the quarried rock is not limestone like the little crag perched above it and the rock strata sweeps up nearly vertically whereas the limestone's is horizontal. The material of the vertical strata is an ancient Silurian slate, a Pre-Cambrian rock found from Settle almost to Horton at the bottom of the valley. Above Horton the valley floor is limestone which is quarried at Horton.

*   *   *

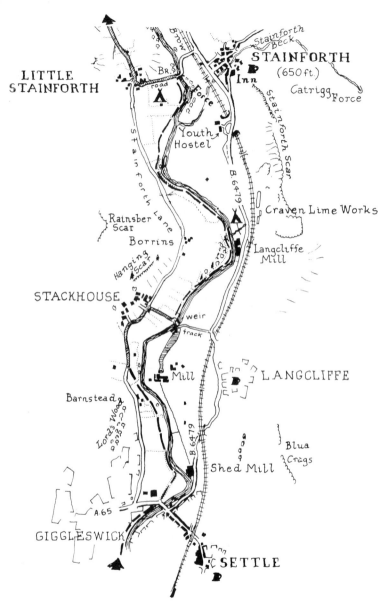

LITTLE
STAINFORTH

STAINFORTH
(650 ft.)

Stainforth Beck

Catrigg Force

Br

road

Stainforth Force

Inn

Youth
Hostel

Stainforth Scar

Stainforth Lane

B 6479

Craven Lime Works

Rainsber
Scar

Borrins

Hanging Scar

Langcliffe
Mill

STACKHOUSE

weir

track

Mill

LANGCLIFFE

Barnstead

Lord's Wood

B 6479

Blua
Crags

Shed Mill

A.65

GIGGLESWICK

SETTLE

90

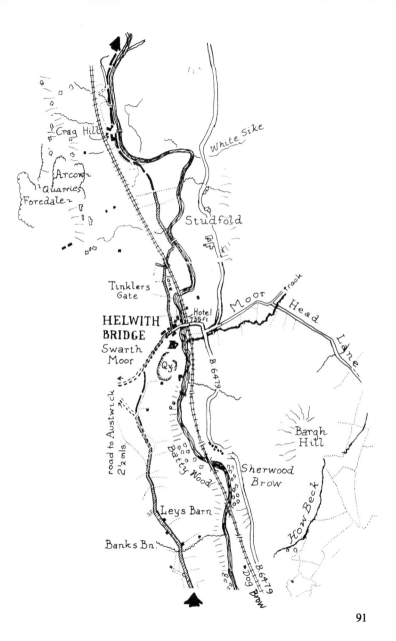

Crag Hill

White Sike

Arcow
Quarries
Foredale

Studfold

Tinklers
Gate

Moor   track   Head   Lane

HELWITH
BRIDGE
Swarth
Moor

Hotel
735ft

Q.y.

B 6479

road to Austwick
2½ mls.

Bargh
Hill

Batty Wood

Sherwood
Brow

How Beck

Leys Barn

Banks Bn.

B 6479
Dog Brow

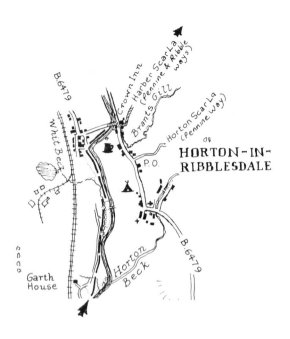

B.6479

Crown Inn

Harber Scar La
(Pennine & Ribble
ways)

Brants Gill

Horton Scar La
(Pennine Way)

HORTON-IN-
RIBBLESDALE

P.O.

Whit Beck

B.6479

Horton
Beck

Garth
House

Pen-y-Ghent from above Horton

SECTION 8
HORTON IN RIBBLESDALE TO THE SOURCE

Facts and facilities
Mileage: 6.5 to Far Gearstones, 10.5 to the source.
Map: 1/25,000 Outdoor Leisure Map. The Three Peaks.

Facilities
Almost non-existent. The Station Hotel at Ribblehead is a good mile away, The Gearstones Inn marked on the above map is no longer a pub

The route
Horton to Gearstones
Turn up the rough lane[1] to the right of the Crown: it is the Pennine Way going north to Hawes. Follow it as far as Sell Gill Barn, about a mile. It is the first building after a sizeable stream, Sell Gill,[2] but note that the stream may be dry in summer. Turn left here through a step-stile and then right immediately below the barn. The path is faint but

93

keep in a straight line through the long fields to find the ladder and stiles and gates. In due course you will come to a short field with ladder stiles leading both in and out. Instead of going over the second one leave the field by the gate on the left. A sizeable gill divides this field. Go round its head on the right and then make gently up to the right to get round the head of the much bigger gill, Birkwith Gill.[3] You will come to a cart-track, follow it until you come to the High Birkwith-Old Ing farm road. Turn right on it and look for a faint path that crosses the small stream and leads to a well marked track that goes to Gods Bridge[4] on Brow Gill Beck. Cross the bridge and stile and bear left round the hill and drop down to Nether Lodge. Cross the stream, Ling Gill and go between the farmhouse and its buildings to reach its access road. Here you will find two finger posts, one of them directing you to Gearstones. The path may be very faint to start with, look for the ladder stile on the distant fence, so far away it is scarcely recognisable as such, but this is where you are aiming for. From this point onwards the path across these rolling[5] hillocks is better marked. It drops down a little to cross Crutchin Gill and climbs up again to a gate. After passing a ruined lime kiln you reach Black Hools Barn*. Go through the gate, pass

*Note. At some future date the route may be changed. Watch for signs indicating a diversion.

God's Bridge

Approaching Birkwith along the limestone shelf. Typical Dales barns are seen. Whernside, shrouded in mist, lies at the head of the valley.

the barn and into the field beyond. Now turn right and follow the wall over the hill to the ruined farmhouse and barn. Here turn right through the gate and immediately turn left and follow the wall to the first bend. Here keep straight on but bear left and climb up to the top of the ridge. The path swings round in a big curve to the left to avoid the very steep descent by the wall to the cattle bridge over Thorns Gill. Across the river a very obvious track leads to the road close to Gearstones,[6] where you turn right on the road.

Gearstones to the source

The road follows the river right to Newby Head but it is no place for walkers. It is far better to use The Dales Way to reach Newby Head. Follow the road for about 300 yards to the cart-track at The Dales Way signpost and follow it as far as Windshaw. You will see a stile on the right between two buildings. Cross it and climb diagonally left up the field to find the next stile. Keep more or less straight across to find the next one, then go through a gate to pass a barn and then High Gayle Farm. Here go through the gate between two large sycamore trees then out onto the open fell at the next gate. Here you rejoin The Dales Way, an extremely boggy cart-track that runs along the edge of the steeper ground to join the Newby Head-Dent road. Turn right here and follow the road to its junction with the Ingleton-Hawes road. Turn right to cross the bridge and at once strike up the fell side for 70-80 yards to find a narrow track, just visible from the road. It develops into a cart-track within a few hundred yards and swings round the shoulder of the fell to end at a concrete hut used to store animal fodder. Here have a good look at the fell and get yourself orientated, for route finding is not easy and as yet the track is barely marked. Looking across the stream you will see high above the rough moor a band of much greener grass. The source of the Ribble lies above the left-hand side of that green band. The left-hand one of two streams (Shiver Gill) seems to run directly to it, but do not follow it. Instead follow the main stream for a time, but take care not to go too far. In less than ½ mile cross the stream and follow the prominent tributary on the right. It curves round to the right and eventually goes underground - for you have now reached the limestone strata - except in winter or wet weather. A number of small springs appear here and there, but keep going up to the wall. Turn right and follow it past a gateway blocked with piled up concrete blocks. Just a little further is the highest spring of all, burbling forth in a most satisfying manner from the foot of a little rocky bank, and running even in summer. This spring, at an altitude of just over 1800ft is surely the true source of the Ribble.

The source of the Ribble

Return to Civilisation
The easiest way back to Horton in Ribblesdale is by the Pennine
Way. (It is of course equally easy to get to Hawes if that suits your
plans.) The problem at the moment is getting to the Pennine Way.
There is a non right-of-way path to it beyond that blocked gateway
but all other possible ways involve crossing unstable limestone walls,
very nasty indeed. The author can only suggest that you retrace your
steps to the road, go down it for a couple of miles and join the
Pennine Way by means of the footpath marked 'Roman Road' on
the Three Peaks map. It is to be hoped that the Yorkshire Dales
National Park will quickly negotiate a right of way path across this
crucial section and place a stile at the gateway.

Things seen on the Way

1. Sell Gill Lane was the original road up the valley and joined the Lancaster-Richmond road on Dodd Fell.

2. In normal weather Sell Gill disappears in the stream bed above the cart-track in a quite dramatic manner forming Sell Gill Pot. This pothole was explored as early as 1897 by the Yorkshire Ramblers Club who found a deep shaft leading into a huge cavern, considered to be Yorkshire's largest - the largest being the Main Chamber of Gaping Gill. Below the road there is another entrance, a cave cum shaft which leads to the same cavern. The pothole has a total depth of 210ft.

3. Birkwith Cave is at the head of the ravine and a sizeable stream issues from it. There is a stile into the ravine on the farm side of it and it is not difficult to get down to the cave, the mouth of which is impressively large, but it quickly becomes impossible. Directly across the valley a small plantation of conifers above Selside marks the position of Alum Pot.

4. God's Bridge is a natural limestone bridge over the deep cut stream, so massive it is hardly recognisable as a bridge.

5. The numerous little hillocks crossed by the Way just after Nether Lodge are drumlins, heaps of debris left by the retreating glaciers of the last Ice Age.

6. In the last days before the railways were built cattle were driven from Scotland to the English markets and Gearstones was one of their resting places.

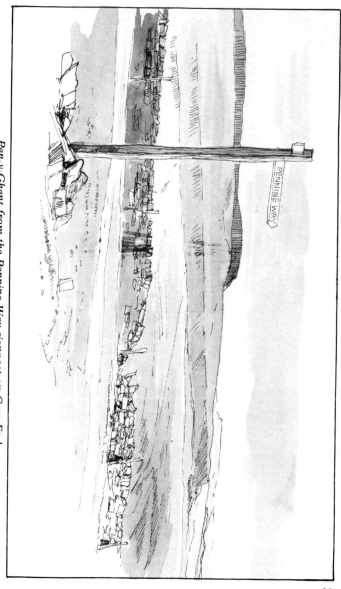

Pen-y-Ghent from the Pennine Way signpost on Cam End

PENNINE WAY

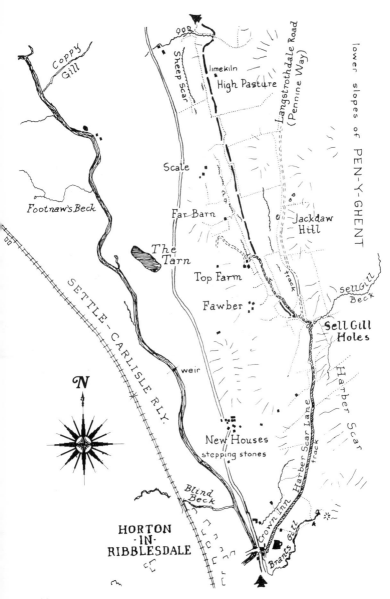

Coppy Gill

Sheep Scar

limekiln

High Pasture

Langstrothdale Road (Pennine Way)

lower slopes of PEN-Y-GHENT

Footnaw's Beck

Scale

Far Barn

The Tarn

Top Farm

Fawber

Jackdaw Hill

track

Sell Gill Beck

Sell Gill Holes

SETTLE - CARLISLE RLY.

weir

N

Harber Scar

New Houses

stepping stones

Harber Scar Lane

track

Blind Beck

HORTON
·IN·
RIBBLESDALE

Crown Inn

Brants Gill

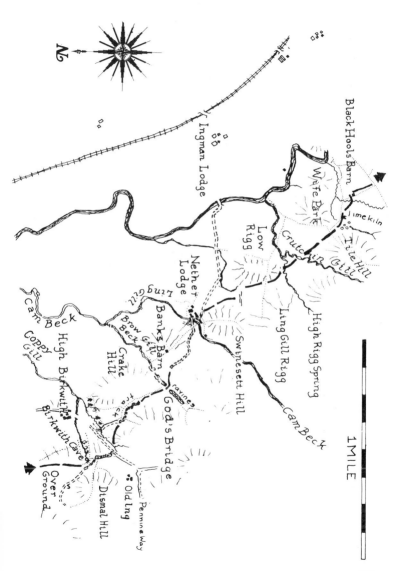

NL

BlackHools Barn

Ingman Lodge

Lime kiln

Wite Park

Tile Hill

Low Rigg

Crutchin Gill

Nether Lodge

Ling Gill Rigg

High Rigg Spring

Ling Gill

Banks Barn

Cam Beck

Crake Hill

Brow Gill Beck

Swinesett Hill

Cam Beck

Coppy Gill

High Birkwith

God's Bridge

ravines

Birkwith Cave

Over Ground

Dismal Hill

Old Ing

Pennine Way

1 MILE

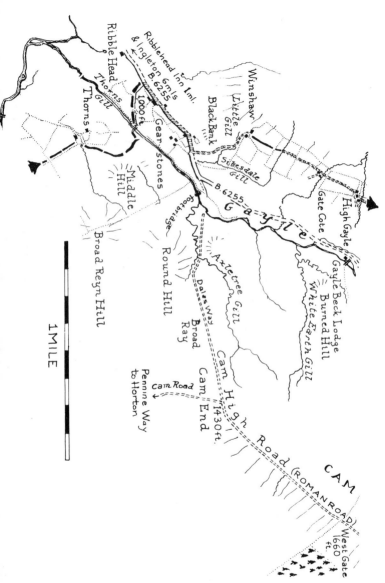

1 MILE

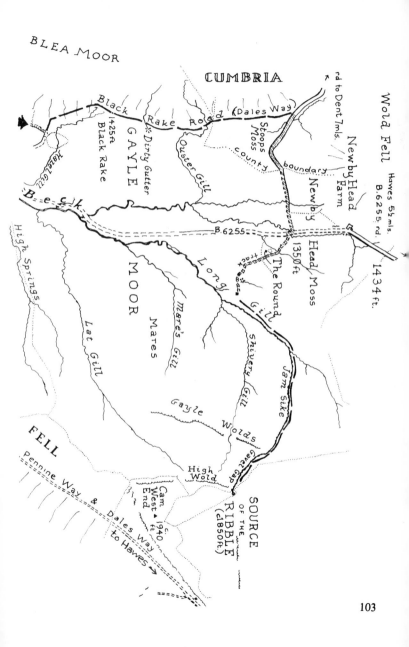

BLEA MOOR

CUMBRIA

rd to Dent 7mls.

BLACK Rake Road (Dales Way)

GAYLE

1425ft.
Black Rake

Dirty Gutter

Ouster Gill

Stoops
Moss

county boundary

Newby Head
Farm

Newby

Wold Fell

Hazel Gill

Beck

B.6255

Long

Gill

Head Moss

The Round

1350ft

Haws track

Hawes 52 mls.
B.6255 rd.

1434ft.

MOOR

High Springs

Lat Gill

Mares

Mare's Gill

Gayle Wolds

Shivery Gill

Jam Sike

High Wold

High Wold

Cave Gap

FELL

Pennine Way

Cam
West
End

1940
ft.

Cave Gap

SOURCE
OF THE
RIBBLE
(c1850ft.)

Dales Way
to Hawes →

103

PRINTED BY
CARNMOR PRINT & DESIGN
95/97 LONDON ROAD, PRESTON